History and Current Condition of Longleaf Pine in the Southern United States

Christopher M. Oswalt, Jason A. Cooper, Dale G. Brockway,
Horace W. Brooks, Joan L. Walker, Kristina F. Connor,
Sonja N. Oswalt, and Roger C. Conner

United States
Department of
Agriculture

Forest Service

Southern
Research Station

General Technical
Report SRS–166

Authors

Christopher M. Oswalt, Research Forester, and **Jason A. Cooper**, Forester, U.S. Department of Agriculture Forest Service, Southern Research Station, Forest Inventory and Analysis, Knoxville, TN 37919; **Dale G. Brockway**, Research Ecologist, U.S. Department of Agriculture Forest Service, Southern Research Station, Restoring and Managing Longleaf Pine Ecosystems, Auburn, AL 36849; **Horace W. Brooks**, Forestry Technician, U.S. Department of Agriculture Forest Service, Southern Research Station, Forest Inventory and Analysis, Knoxville, TN 37919; **Joan L. Walker**, Research Plant Ecologist, U.S. Department of Agriculture Forest Service, Southern Research Station, Restoring and Managing Longleaf Pine Ecosystems, Clemson, SC 29634; **Kristina F. Connor**, Project Leader, U.S. Department of Agriculture Forest Service, Southern Research Station, Restoring and Managing Longleaf Pine Ecosystems, Auburn, AL 36849; **Sonja N. Oswalt**, Forester, and **Roger C. Conner**, Research Forester (retired), U.S. Department of Agriculture Forest Service, Southern Research Station, Forest Inventory and Analysis, Knoxville, TN 37919.

Cover photos: top left, a longleaf pine forest in Louisiana treated with the shelterwood method (residual basal area 25–30 square feet per acre). (photo by Bill Boyer, U.S. Forest Service); top right, foliage and cones of longleaf pine (*Pinus palustris*). (photo by Erich G. Vallery, U.S. Forest Service); bottom, *Pinus palustris* regeneration, Wambaw Ranger District, Francis Marion National Forest, North Carolina. (photo by Bill Lea).

November 2012

History and Current Condition of Longleaf Pine in the Southern United States

Christopher M. Oswalt, Jason A. Cooper, Dale G. Brockway, Horace W. Brooks, Joan L. Walker, Kristina F. Connor, Sonja N. Oswalt, and Roger C. Conner

Mature open stand of *Pinus palustris*, Carolina Sandhills National Wildlife Refuge, Chesterfield County, South Carolina. (photo by Jack Culpepper, U.S. Fish and Wildlife Service)

Contents

Author Contributions

Christopher M. Oswalt as primary author, contributed all analyses, text, tables, and figures not attributed to another author, provided initial edits, facilitated external reviews, and provided two revisions of the report.

Jason A. Cooper contributed analysis, text, tables, and figures for the Productive Capacity of Longleaf Pine section and aided editing and revisions.

Dale G. Brockway contributed the History of Longleaf Pine in the South section and provided considerable editing support.

Horace W. Brooks contributed all mapped products not attributed to another author and acted as the primary map builder for this project.

Joan L. Walker contributed the Ecology of Longleaf Pine Forest Communities section.

Kristina F. Connor provided the Future Research Needs section.

Sonja N. Oswalt contributed text, tables, and figures covering the distribution of invasive plants.

Roger C. Conner (retired) contributed the Methods section.

History and Current Condition of Longleaf Pine in the Southern United States

Christopher M. Oswalt, Jason A. Cooper, Dale G. Brockway, Horace W. Brooks, Joan L. Walker, Kristina F. Connor, Sonja N. Oswalt, and Roger C. Conner

Abstract

Longleaf pine (*Pinus palustris* Mill.) was once one of the most ecologically important tree species in the Southern United States. Longleaf pine and its accompanying forest ecosystems covered vast swaths of the Southern United States, spanning an estimated 92 million acres. Although once one of the most extensive forest ecosystems in North America, only a fraction of these longleaf pine forests remain today. Here we present a brief description of longleaf pine ecosystems and their constituent parts, a history of longleaf pine in the South, and the recent historical and current status of longleaf pine forests as sampled by the U.S. Department of Agriculture Forest Service Forest Inventory and Analysis program. We present estimated changes to the longleaf pine forests, implications for conservation of the species, and suggestions for future research. While longleaf pine dominated forests have received considerable attention and land managers and conservation professionals are working to maintain and improve these important systems, longleaf pine forests currently only occupy a minor portion of the southern landscape. There are positive signs in this report, however, that point toward potential improvements. For example, the number of longleaf pine saplings has been increasing, the longleaf pine/oak acreage represents a considerable opportunity for restoration to longleaf pine forests, and in some areas of the longleaf pine range young stands are developing to aid replacement of those lost. Significant challenges to expanding the coverage of longleaf pine dominated forests do exist. However, with targeted research and conservation efforts, longleaf pine forests can thrive once again across the South.

Keywords: FIA, forest inventory, longleaf pine, pine conservation, *Pinus palustris*, southern pines.

Longleaf pine (*Pinus palustris*) at Royal Botanic Gardens Melbourne. (photo by Peter Halasz)

Introduction

Longleaf pine (*Pinus palustris* Mill.) was once one of the most ecologically important tree species in the Southern United States. Longleaf pine and its accompanying forest ecosystems covered vast swaths of the Southern United States, spanning an estimated 60–90 million acres. One estimate places the historical extent of longleaf pine forests at 92 million acres (Frost 2006). Although once one of the most extensive forest ecosystems in North America, only a fraction of these longleaf pine forests remain today.

It is imperative that longleaf pine, a high-priority conservation species and forest ecosystem, receive continuous focused monitoring. The Forest Inventory and Analysis (FIA) program of the Forest Service, U.S. Department of Agriculture, is the only program currently positioned to provide continuous and unbiased range-wide (large-scale) monitoring of this important

resource. The remaining longleaf pines are scarce when compared to their historical extent, and are spread among eight Southern States in largely fragmented stands (longleaf pine is known to historically and currently occur in southeastern Virginia, however does not currently occur in the FIA sample used for this report). Much of this remaining acreage is thought by scientists, conservationists, and land managers to be in poor condition. Numerous large-scale conservation efforts are currently underway (e.g., see America's Longleaf—www.americaslongleaf.org) with the goal of conserving and improving existing stands, and increasing the extent of longleaf pine forests across the South. This report can help establish a baseline that may be used to better understand and evaluate the impact and/ or effectiveness of large-scale (range-wide) conservation efforts.

Here we present a brief description of longleaf pine ecosystems and their constituent parts, a history of longleaf pine in the South, and the recent historical and current status of longleaf pine forests as sampled by the FIA program. We also discuss changes to the longleaf pine forests, implications for conservation of the species, and suggestions for future research.

Ecology of Longleaf Pine Forest Communities

High quality longleaf pine systems, throughout their range, are generally described as containing widely spaced overstory longleaf pines over a predominantly herbaceous ground layer dominated by grasses and a diverse mixture of showy forbs. Woody species, if present in the ground layer, are short and inconspicuous. At a glance, this ecosystem appears to be simple—pines over grasses. This simplified picture, however, belies the remarkable botanical diversity within the longleaf pine ecosystem. Some longleaf pine woodlands, ranking among the most diverse in North America, contain >40 vascular plant species in 1 m² (Walker and Peet 1983) or 170 per 1,000 m² (Peet and others 2006, Carr and others 2010). The diversity of this once extensive ecosystem is also represented in the many types of longleaf-dominated communities that have been described. Peet (2006) recognized 135 longleaf pine vegetation associations.

The canopy dominance of longleaf pine and the importance of fire are unifying characteristics of diverse longleaf pine ecosystems. Frequent, low intensity surface fires are critical for maintaining a vigorous ground layer. Grasses, legumes, and composites are the most common plant families in these fire-dependent habitats (Harcombe and others 1993, Peet and Allard 1993, Drew and others 1998). Most of the common species are sun-loving perennials with the ability to resprout after fire. Fire typically stimulates the flowering and seed production of many characteristic species, and there are apt to be species flowering at most any time during the growing season. Over time, the reduction of fire disturbance on the landscape has contributed to the reduced extent and altered conditions of longleaf pine ecosystems across the region.

Despite these commonalities, there is considerable variation from one part of the region to another. Most herbaceous species have smaller geographic ranges than longleaf pine. Species with restricted geographic ranges are referred to as endemic, and the longleaf pine ecosystem has many subregional and local endemic species (Estill and Cruzan 2001, LeBlond 2001, Sorrie and Weakley 2006). As the geographic limit of a species' range is reached, it drops out of the local flora but may be replaced by an ecologically similar species. The result is an altered species composition in the ground layer. Species with very small geographic distributions (narrow endemics) are prone to extinction and include some of ground layer species that are federally listed as threatened or endangered (Walker 1999).

Overall, longleaf pine ecosystems consist of sparse to open canopies dominated by longleaf pine, occasionally mixed

A surface fire moving through a longleaf pine/wiregrass understory in southern Georgia. Prescribed fire is an essential ecological process for restoration and maintenance of longleaf pine ecosystems. (photo by Ron Masters, Tall Timbers Station, Florida)

An uneven-aged longleaf pine forest growing on a xeric sandhill in northern Florida that has been well maintained by frequent fire. (photo by Dale Brockway, U.S. Forest Service)

with shortleaf (*P. echinata*), slash (*P. elliottii*), or pond pine (*P. serotina*). Tree boles typically appear blackened by fire activity, and there is usually little forest floor or litter accumulation (a consequence of frequent burning). The high open canopy and shallow litter and duff layers provide conditions needed to support vigorous ground layer vegetation. In frequently burned sites there is normally no midstory, so sufficient light reaches the understory to support a prairie-like herbaceous ground layer. In some circumstances, the ground layer may contain varying amounts of low woody vegetation including hardwood seedlings and shrubs.

The most recent comprehensive description of longleaf pine vegetation recognizes six general types based on soil moisture and texture as described below. These types represent generalized communities with variations of each found in most parts of the longleaf pine range. The following descriptions are based on the best remaining examples of the types, sites presumably burned frequently in recent decades and without a history of intensive agriculture, along with some historical references (Peet 2006).

Xeric sand barrens and uplands—Vegetation on the driest, deepest sands consists of scattered pines with a scrubby oak understory. Turkey oak (*Quercus laevis*) is the most common oak on xeric sites through most of the

longleaf pine range. The ground layer may have patches of small shrubs and mats of lichens, but grass and forb cover is sparse. Bare sand is common. Fires would have occurred infrequently because fuels are discontinuous and slow to accumulate between fires. With fire exclusion, oaks increase, shading the sparse grasses.

Subxeric sandy uplands—Subxeric sites hold enough moisture to support a wider variety of upland oaks, as well as a continuous grassy ground layer. Oaks may include turkey oak, but also bluejack oak (*Q. incana*), sand post oak (*Q. margarettiae*), sand live oak (*Q. geminate*), and dwarf live oak (*Q. minima*). Wiregrasses (*Aristida stricta* or *A. beyrichiana*) dominate within their ranges and bluestems (*Andropogon* spp. and *Schizachyrium* spp.) elsewhere. Subxeric types occur in the fall-line sandhills, as well as in the outer coastal plain sometimes described as dry flatwoods. These sites may support a variety of grasses in addition to wiregrass, and in some areas unique forbs.

Silty uplands—Longleaf pine on silty uplands is rare, as these sites were choice agricultural sites for early settlers. Based on historical accounts and remnant fragments, these woodlands were rich in species, especially legumes and composites, and little bluestem was ubiquitous. The productive soils yielded lush and continuous herbaceous cover.

Clayey and rock uplands—Longleaf pine-type vegetation occurred on a variety of clayey and rocky substrates ranging from thin sands over ironstone or on exposed marine shrink-swell clay soils. Characteristic oaks include blackjack (*Q. marilandica*) and post oaks (*Q. stellata*), more characteristic of Piedmont forests. Piedmont and montane longleaf pine occurs mostly on exposed ridges and south-facing slopes, similar to surrounding upland forests. Longleaf pine occurs with shortleaf pines, oaks, and other upland hardwoods. The herbaceous layer is dominated by wiregrass and includes some species such as creeping blueberry (*Vaccinium crassifolium*) and pixie moss (*V. crassifolium*) usually associated with clay soils, as well as species common to surrounding sandy sites.

Flatwoods—Longleaf pine clearly dominates these sites on the Atlantic coastal plain, but can be mixed with slash pine in the southern range. Generally speaking, flatwoods do not have significant oak components except for running oaks (*Q. pumila* and *Q. minima*). The abundance of palmetto (*Serenoa repens*) and its codominance with wiregrass, bracken fern (*Pteridium aquilinum* var. *pseudocaudatum*), and runner oaks, contribute to the distinctive appearance of flatwoods vegetation. Some drier sites may include additional scrub oaks in the understory or shrub layer where they may mix with shrubs such as gallberry (*Ilex glabra*), dwarf huckleberry (*Gaylussacia dumosa*), and wax myrtle (*Morella pumila*). The forb component of southern flatwoods is diverse, but legumes are uncommon.

Savannas, seeps, and prairies—These types occur on wet, fine-textured (silty) soils through the longleaf pine range. The pine canopy is very open and may include slash and pond pines along with longleaf pine. They are widely recognized for high levels of species richness. The herb layer is rich in grasses and sedges, and is well-known for the diversity of orchids, carnivorous plants, and other showy species. Legumes, however, are conspicuously scarce. The sites are typically wet and can occur as large broad expanses in the outer coastal plain and as small patches associated with stream heads in the fall-line sandhills.

History of Longleaf Pine in the South

During the most recent Ice Age [≅40,000 to 12,000 years before present (BP)], forests in the southern region consisted of boreal elements (*Picea, Pinus*) and temperate species (*Carya, Castanea, Ostrya, Quercus*) intermixed in a pattern that varied both spatially and temporally with the ebb and flow of the vast ice sheet farther to the north (Watts 1970, Delcourt 1980, Watts and others 1992). As the continental glacier retreated (after 12,000 years BP), southern forests became dominated by oaks and a diverse array of deciduous hardwoods (Watts 1971, Watts and Hansen 1988, Watts and others 1992). Longleaf pine expanded northward and eastward from its Ice Age refuge in southern Texas and northern Mexico (Schmidtling and Hipkins 1998) and became established in the lower coastal plain about 8,000 years ago (Watts and others 1992). During the ensuing 4,000 years, longleaf pine continued to spread throughout the Southeast (Delcourt and Delcourt 1987).

This several thousand years, pre-Columbian time period coincides with the interval during which populations of Native Americans flourished throughout the region, and their use of fire is thought to be related to the development and maintenance of longleaf pine forest ecosystems (Schwartz 1994, Pyne 1997, Landers and Boyer 1999). Because of these natural and anthropogenic interactions, longleaf pine forests became one of the most extensive ecosystems in North America (Landers and others 1995), occupying about 92 million acres in the Southeastern United States (Frost 2006). The native range of longleaf pine extended along the Gulf and Atlantic Coastal Plains from Texas to Virginia, and well into central Florida and the piedmont and mountains of northern Alabama and northwestern Georgia, from sea level to elevations around 2,000 feet (Boyer 1990, Stout and Marion 1993, Stowe and others 2002). Travelers in this region during the 18th and 19th centuries noted vast areas where longleaf pine covered >90 percent of the landscape (Bartram 1791, Williams 1837).

Native Americans frequently used fire to manipulate their environment (Robbins and Myers 1992, Anderson 1996, Carroll and others 2002, Stanturf and others 2002, Frost 2006), and early settlers adopted the practice of periodically burning nearby forests and woodlands to improve forage quality for cattle grazing and discourage the encroachment of woody undergrowth. Although well adapted to surface fires at a naturally-occurring frequency of 2–3 years (Brockway and Lewis 1997), longleaf pine was not well adapted to other disturbances introduced by early settlers. The cumulative impacts of three centuries of changing land use resulted in the dramatic decline of longleaf pine forests, and they have become one of the most endangered ecosystems in the United States (Noss and others 1995).

Habitat loss principally resulted from conversion of longleaf pine forests to other uses (i.e., agriculture, industrial pine plantations, and urban development), landscape fragmentation, and interruption of natural fire regimes (Landers and others 1995, Wear and Greis 2002). English colonization of the longleaf pine range began during the 17th century, with concerted immigration efforts to settle and commercially develop lands along the Atlantic Coastal Plain from Virginia to Georgia and subsequently the Piedmont. Beginning in the 16th century, Spanish domination of the area from Florida to Texas largely blocked settlement of the gulf coast interior, leaving many of the region's longleaf pine forests in pristine condition well into the 19th century, when the area was incorporated into the United States (Frost 2006). Although the Spanish did not encourage immigration to and settlement of this region, Americans, modeling their development pattern after the commercial ventures of the English, widely settled these lands (Frost 2006). Dependence on water for travel and trade limited early settlements to coastal areas and lands along rivers and streams (Hart 1979). Without machinery, timber was commercially worth little, except for use in local construction. Therefore, the effects of settlement on longleaf pine forests were initially minor, with harvesting limited to areas near early towns and villages where log structures were constructed (Croker 1987). Later, lumber was cut from longleaf pine logs using hand-powered pitsaws, which yielded only a few rough boards per day (Hindle 1975).

Longleaf pine in Ocala National Forest, Florida. (photo by Bill Lea)

By the mid-1700s, water-powered sawmills became common but log transportation was inefficient and still largely confined to water courses (Frost 1993), with logging conducted on 3-mile-wide strips along rivers where logs could be dragged by oxen or horses and floated to the mill (Croker 1987). This limited harvesting so much that by 1800 most longleaf pine forests remained intact. After 1830, removal of longleaf pine accelerated significantly with the arrival of steam railroads, which were soon followed by the use of steam skidders. By 1880, most of the longleaf pine along streams and railroads had been harvested (Frost 2006). During the next 40 years, the great forests of yellow pine were harvested, with temporary railroad spur lines laid down every quarter mile (Croker 1987). Skidders dragged logs to these spur lines, often destroying all trees too small to harvest, and left a scarred and mostly barren landscape. Longleaf pine forests were harvested from Virginia and the Carolinas, south to Georgia and Florida, then west through Alabama and Mississippi, into Louisiana, and finally Texas. During 1896, 392 million cubic feet of yellow pine timber was cut and shipped to the Northern United States and overseas markets (Mohr 1897). Timber extraction peaked in 1907, when 1.4 billion cubic feet were removed (Wahlenberg 1946). By 1930, nearly all old-growth longleaf pine was harvested and lumber companies migrated west.

Extraction of naval stores (i.e., tar, pitch, rosin, and turpentine derived from pine resin) by cutting wound faces in the bark of longleaf pine trees began in 1608 with the first European settlements in Virginia (Frost 2006). Although substitutes eventually became available in the mid-19th century, naval stores extraction in the South continued until the 20th century, when it was finally supplanted by the petroleum industry (Frost 1993). Because the pitch-soaked faces on these trees would readily ignite, many forests where extraction occurred in this manner were destroyed by wildfire following abandonment. About two-thirds of the sites where longleaf pine was harvested or burned by wildfires following naval stores extraction were later colonized by other tree species. Loblolly pine (*P. taeda*), a prolific seed producer, captured mesic coastal plain sites; slash pine invaded wetter flatwoods areas; and shortleaf pine and hardwoods became dominant on upland sites. Irregular seed production, with good seed years occurring at intervals of 5 years or more (Boyer 1990), impaired longleaf pine recovery and contributed to these losses. Even where

longleaf pine seedlings survived logging, they were often consumed by introduced feral hogs (*Sus scrofa*), causing many areas of potential longleaf pine forests to be lost (Schwarz 1907). Large areas of longleaf pine forests were also converted to agriculture, beginning with early settlers who, like the Native American farmers before them, began by girdling trees and planting crops between dead standing snags. The settlers later burned the snags and burned or dug out the stumps. Annual burning to improve forage for livestock grazing frequently eliminated newly germinated longleaf pine seedlings. Between 1750 and 1850, most of the more fertile longleaf pine sites were converted to fields or pastures (Williams 1989), thereby removing longleaf pine from the best upland areas. Many of these lands were plowed and became cotton plantations (Frost 2006). Although most of the sandhills, flatwoods, and mountain soils are poorly suited for agriculture, some were converted to pasture (Landers and others 1990). Florida was an exception, where sandhill sites are well suited for citrus fruit production (Mohr 1897).

By the late 19th century, it became apparent that longleaf pine was not successfully regenerating on most cutover lands (Mohr 1897). These lands were instead becoming occupied by less-desirable second-growth tree species and, in some cases, remaining open and nearly treeless (Frost 2006). By 1900, logging, harvest of naval stores, and agriculture had reduced the area dominated by longleaf pine by more than one-half (Frost 1993). Logging continued until only fragments of the original longleaf pine forests remained in 1935. Second-growth longleaf pine stands became established on only one-third of the sites previously occupied (Wahlenberg 1946).

Harvesting second-growth longleaf pine became an established practice during the 1940s and continued through the 1980s (Kelly and Bechtold 1990). The construction of pulpmills during the 1950s created an increased demand for smaller trees. These developments accelerated conversion of naturally-regenerated longleaf pine forests into plantations of species that grow more rapidly in the short term. Because of its slower early growth and lower survival rate, longleaf pine was seldom selected to reforest harvested lands. Thus, many second-growth longleaf pine stands on public land and private industrial lands were clearcut, mechanically site prepared, and planted with loblolly pine or slash pine

A second-growth, even-aged longleaf pine forest in southern Alabama on forest industry land. (photo by Bill Boyer, U.S. Forest Service)

(Schultz 1997). Nonindustrial private landowners often relied on natural regeneration following harvest and, because of insufficient longleaf pine seed, many of these sites regenerated into loblolly pine or slash pine forests. Old fields were also planted with these more rapidly growing species or colonized by them through seeding from adjacent areas. This resulted in a continuing decline in the area occupied by longleaf pine ecosystems through the 1990s, when they occupied <5 percent of their original range (Outcalt and Sheffield 1996). Substantial future losses on private lands remain possible, since most of the current longleaf pine stands consist of trees in the valuable sawtimber and pole size-classes.

Reduction in the frequency of fire further contributed to conversion of longleaf pine lands to other species. Extensive logging during the late 19th and early 20th centuries created very heavy loads of downed fuel, and this fuel supported numerous large wildfires that caused many areas to be devoid of trees. Foresters then began to advocate excluding all fire from the woods to protect young trees and allow for reestablishment of the forest. Although some individuals recognized the natural and essential role of fire in longleaf

pine ecosystems (Harper 1913), most people viewed fire as harmful. Since fire control practices aided in establishment of new forests, even though they were usually loblolly pine or slash pine, these procedures were adopted as "good forestry practices" throughout the region (Frost 1993).

Young hardwoods are quite susceptible to mortality from fire, and frequent fires typically limit hardwoods to a small stature in longleaf pine stands (Landers and others 1990, Brockway and Lewis 1997). Occasionally, random variation in fires or protective microsite conditions allowed hardwood stems to survive several fires and become large enough to resist future surface fires (Rebertus and others 1993). Thus, scattered hardwood trees occurred in the canopy or subcanopy of longleaf-dominated forests (Greenberg and Simons 1999). However, in the absence of fire, hardwoods are able to quickly emerge from the understory and form a dense midstory that shades out herbaceous species and longleaf pine seedlings (Brockway and Outcalt 2000, Brockway and others 2009). Without frequent fire, hardwoods will ascend to eventually dominate the overstory, degrading sites not captured by other pines (Outcalt and Brockway 2010). Although the importance of fire in

7

maintaining a healthy longleaf pine ecosystem is now widely recognized, many forests on private lands are still not burned regularly. Recent burning rates on private lands range from a high of 48 percent in Georgia to a low of only 15 percent in North Carolina (Outcalt 2000). Some stands are difficult to burn because they are close to urban areas and highways. Smoke from fires in such locations can have costly offsite effects. This problem is likely to grow worse as population growth creates more wildland-urban interface (WUI) zones, or the zones of transition between unoccupied land and human development. Also, longleaf pine stands on private lands are sometimes small, and this makes burning them more expensive. Because of infrequent burning, many private lands containing longleaf pine are likely to suffer further habitat degradation. A major threat to the remaining longleaf pine is the absence of frequent fire, which results in encroachment by fire-intolerant pines, hardwoods, saw-palmetto (*Serenoa repens*) and other understory shrub species.

Since the arrival of early settlers, lands supporting longleaf pine have also been lost to urban and residential uses. From 1987 to 1995, conversion of longleaf pine land in Florida to other uses resulted in loss of 92,000 acres of these ecosystems. During this 8-year period, about 7,400 acres per year were converted from longleaf pine to urban uses and 3,700 acres per year were lost to agriculture (Outcalt 1998). Similar losses occurred in Georgia, while losses in North Carolina and South Carolina were about one-half this rate. Future growth of the regional population and expected expansion of industrial plantations will likely result in a continuing decline of longleaf pine ecosystems on private lands.

Longleaf pine ecosystems have been very important in the Southern United States, by providing an environmental setting and raw materials for social and economic development in this region. Wild game, forage grasses, wood, and naval stores were the principal products of these forests (Franklin 1997). During the early 20th century, affluent landowners, recognizing the value of longleaf pine forests as habitat for bobwhite quail (*Colinus virginianus*) and whitetail deer (*Odocoileus virginianus*), acquired large tracts to serve as hunting plantations. Many large areas of longleaf pine forests exist today because of the opportunities for hunting and timber harvesting provided on such lands. Although longleaf pine forests were valued by society, human activities played a major role in their decline, with economic exploitation continuing until the future of these ecosystems appeared quite bleak.

Recently, a combination of developments provides new hope that the negative trend for longleaf pine forests can be reversed. Public policy has changed to more strongly support implementation of cooperative efforts for achieving the restoration and sustainable management of longleaf pine forests (U.S. Department of Agriculture and others 2010). Conversion of longleaf pine to other tree species has slowed as numerous Federal and State agencies have begun regenerating longleaf pine on their lands following harvest. The presence of longleaf pine on public lands has begun to increase as a result of concerted efforts to establish new stands and restore degraded longleaf pine forests with prescribed fire, midstory thinning, and other appropriate techniques (Hilliard 1998, McMahon and others 1998, Brockway and Outcalt 2000, Provencher and others 2001, Brockway and others 2009). Interest in longleaf pine reforestation on private lands has surged recently because of financial incentives to private landowners provided by the Federal Government. The southern forestry community has also gained an improved understanding of the ecological value of longleaf pine ecosystems and come to appreciate the natural heritage that will be lost if restoration of these ecosystems is not undertaken (Darden and others 2009, Diop and others 2009).

Objectives of this Report

The objectives of this report are:

1. To provide a comprehensive assessment of the status of longleaf pine forests in the Southeastern United States,

2. To outline historical and recent changes to the longleaf pine resource, and

3. To provide a solid baseline of information in which future comparisons can be made in order to assess the impact of ongoing rangewide longleaf pine forest restoration activities.

Methods

The Forest Inventory and Analysis Inventory

Historical and contemporary data from the national FIA program of the U.S. Forest Service (Frayer and Furnival 2000, Bechtold and Patterson 2005) was examined. The FIA program is the primary source for information about the extent, condition, status, and trends of forest resources across all ownerships in the United States (Smith and others 2001). Today, FIA applies a nationally consistent sampling protocol using a quasi-systematic design covering all ownerships in the entire Nation (Bechtold and Patterson 2005). FIA operates a multiphase inventory based on an array of hexagons assigned to separate interpenetrating, nonoverlapping annual sampling panels (Bechtold and Patterson 2005). In phase 1, land area is stratified using aerial photography or classified satellite imagery to increase the precision of estimates using stratified estimation. In phase 2, one permanent fixed-area plot is installed in each hexagon that contains accessible forest land and meets FIA specifications. Data is collected for >300 variables across multiple scales (e.g., plot, subplot, condition, and tree) (U.S. Department of Agriculture Forest Service 2008). Plot intensity for phase 2 measurements is about one plot for every 6,000 acres of land (roughly 125,000 plots nationally).

The plot design for FIA inventory plots consists of four 24.0 feet fixed-radius subplots spaced 120 feet apart in a triangular arrangement with one subplot in the center. All trees, with a diameter at breast height (d.b.h.) of at least 5 inches, are inventoried on forested subplots. Within each subplot, a 6.8-feet radius microplot offset 12 feet from subplot center is established. Within each microplot, all-live tree seedlings are tallied according to species. Additionally, all trees with a d.b.h. between 1.0 and 5.0 inches are inventoried. Conifer seedlings must be at least 6 inches in height with a root collar diameter <1 inch. Hardwood seedlings must be at least 12 inches in height with a root collar diameter <1 inch.

Data

All inventory data are made publicly accessible through the FIA database (FIADB). Data for this report were taken from the FIADB (Woudenberg and others 2010). Data were available and compiled for four points in time—1970s, 1980s, 1990s, and current (2010)—and consisted of variable inventory dates (table 1). Data collected prior to 1999 were

Table 1—Periodic and annual inventory dates labeled by State and decade

State	Decade			2010
	1970	1980	1990	
	- - - periodic - - -			annual
Alabama	1972	1982	1990	2010
Florida	1970	1980	1995	2010
Georgia	1972	1982	1997	2010
Louisiana	1974	1984	1991	2009
Mississippi	1977	1987	1994	2010
North Carolina	1974	1984	1990	2010
South Carolina	1978	1986	1993	2010
East Texas	1975	1986	1992	2010

collected under the periodic inventory design while data collected from 1999 to the present have been collected using the annual inventory design (see Bechtold and Patterson 2005). (Note: for a detailed description of current and past data collection and estimate derivation procedures see the appendix.)

Longleaf pine is prevalent in two FIA-defined forest-type groups, loblolly-shortleaf pine and oak-pine as the longleaf pine and longleaf pine/oak forest types, respectively. These forest-type groups and individual forest types are defined by the proportion of total stocking represented by various pine species and their associates. The longleaf pine type is defined as forests in which pines account for at least 50 percent of the stocking of all-live trees, with longleaf pine the most common pine. The mixed longleaf pine/oak forest type are those plots in which pine species account for 25 to 50 percent of total stocking and longleaf pine is the dominant pine species. For the purposes of this report, longleaf pine dominated forests are defined as forests belonging to both the longleaf pine and longleaf pine/oak forest types. References to specific forest types, such as the longleaf pine forest type, will always be explicit.

Summarized estimates are presented for both timberland (forested land available for timber production) and forest land. Timberland estimates were used for analyzing long-term trends due to the historical availability of estimates and the relative stability of the FIA definition of timberland. Forest land estimates (all forest-covered lands according to the FIA definition, (Woudenberg and others 2010) were used to assess current condition and recent changes (for example, estimates of growth, removals, and mortality).

Findings

Extent of Longleaf Pine Forests

According to data collected by the FIA program from the 1970s to current (2010), the population of longleaf pine trees in the Southern United States is still declining. During the 1970s the geographic extent of longleaf pine (or "footprint" of longleaf pine) sampled by the FIA program closely resembled that of the range documented by Little (1971) (fig. 1). Data collected just a decade later indicated that longleaf pine loss was occurring and that the longleaf pine footprint in the South continued to shrink (fig. 2). A comparison of data collected during the 1970s with that of data collected during the 1990s illustrates further loss of longleaf pine (fig. 3). Loss of areal extent appeared to be focused largely in the northern reaches of the East Coastal Plain in North Carolina and the western reaches of the Piedmont in northern Alabama. The most current FIA data collected illustrates continued contraction of the geographic extent of longleaf pine in the South (fig. 4). With few exceptions, the footprint of longleaf pine sampled by FIA is apparently contracting along the borders of the entire range.

The most recent data indicates a much smaller geographic extent for longleaf pine than even as recently as the 1970s (fig. 5). Currently, longleaf pine, while still found in eight Southern States, covers far less acreage than it once did. According to Frost (2006), excluding recently established plantations; longleaf pine had been extirpated from all but 2.6 million acres or about 2.2 percent of its original range by 2005.

Inventory data indicate the current extent of longleaf dominated forests (longleaf pine and longleaf pine/ oak forest types combined) in the South is an estimated 4.3 million acres (table 2) and was observed in Alabama, Florida, Georgia, Louisiana, Mississippi, North Carolina, South Carolina, and Texas (fig. 6). Of the 216 million acres of total forest land area in the South, the longleaf pine forest type makes up only 3.3 million acres, or 1.5 percent

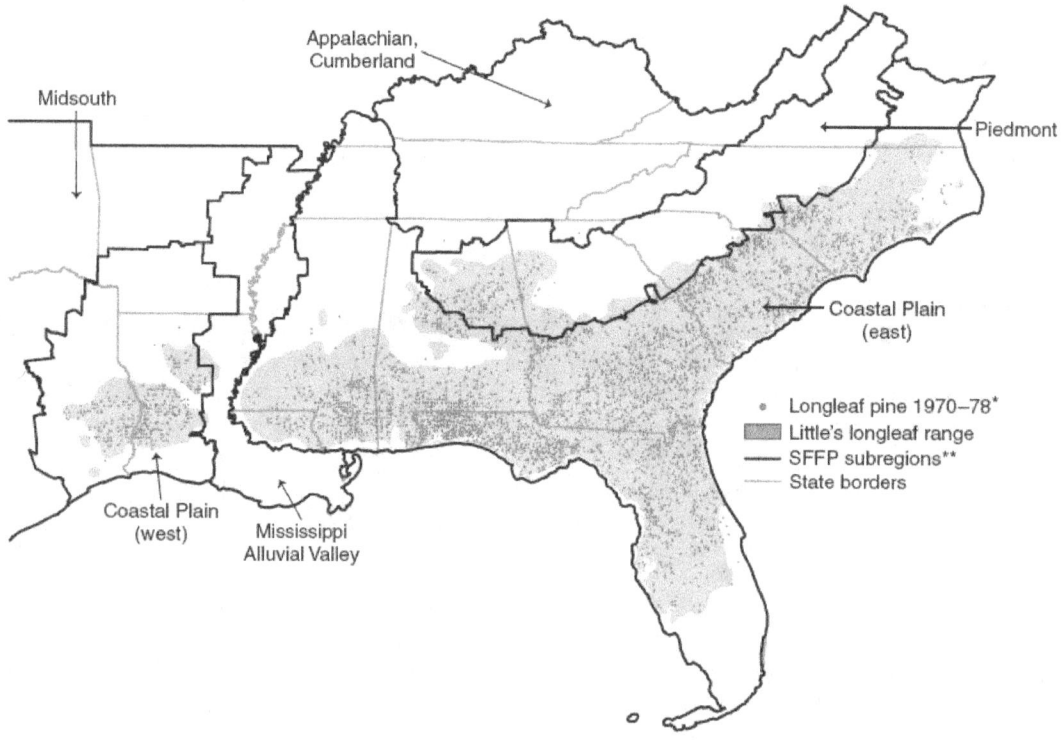

* Plot locations are approximate.
** Southern Forests Futures Project delineations (Wear and others 2009).

Figure 1—Approximate location of longleaf pine sampled by the Forest Inventory and Analysis program 1970–78 as compared to the documented longleaf pine range (Little 1971).

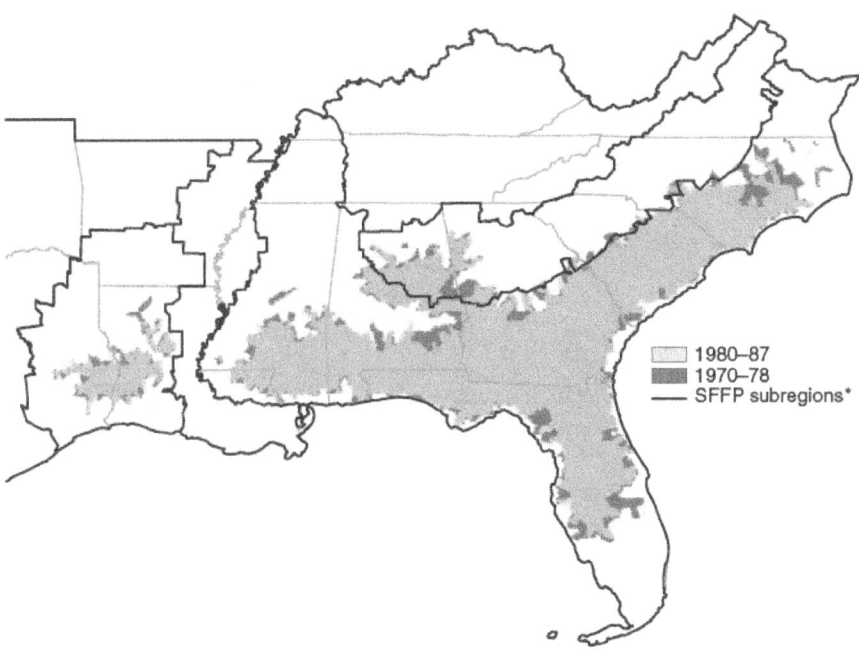

* Southern Forests Futures Project delineations (Wear and others 2009).

Figure 2—Geographic extent of longleaf pine sampled by the Forest Inventory and Analysis program 1980–87 as compared to 1970–78.

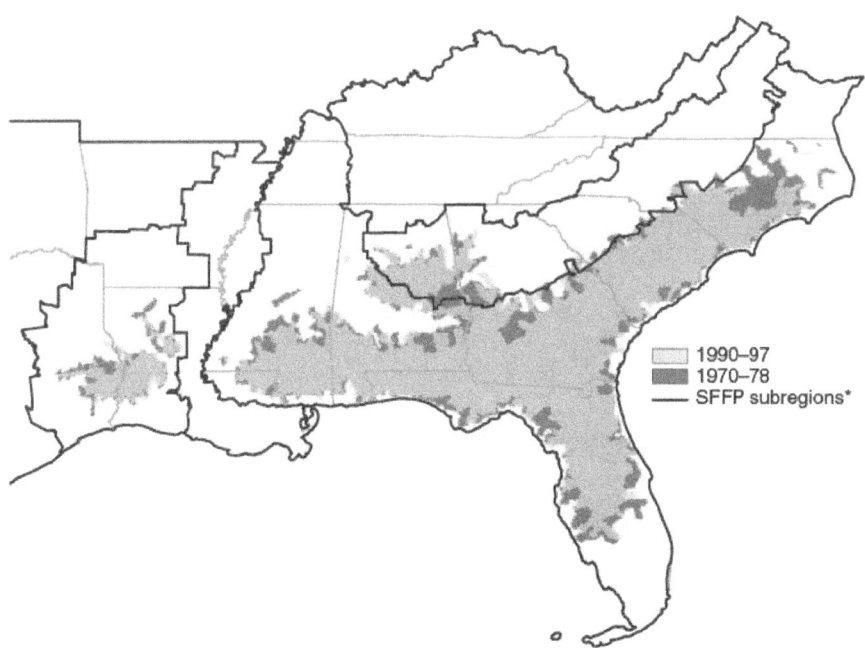

* Southern Forests Futures Project delineations (Wear and others 2009).

Figure 3—Geographic extent of longleaf pine sampled by the Forest Inventory and Analysis program 1990–97 as compared to 1970–78.

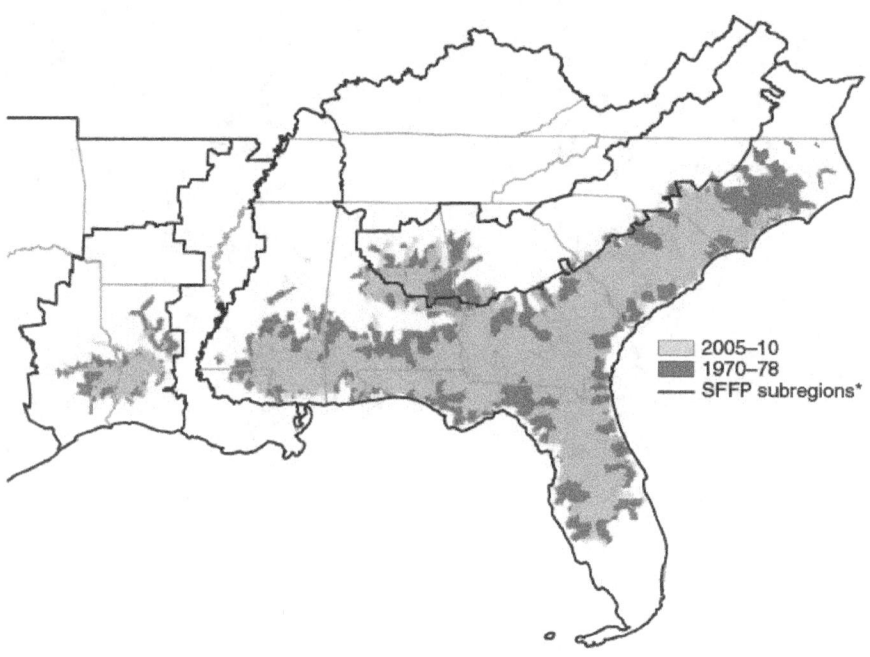

2005–10
1970–78
— SFFP subregions*

* Southern Forests Futures Project delineations (Wear and others 2009).

Figure 4—Geographic extent of longleaf pine sampled by the Forest Inventory and Analysis program 2005–10 as compared to 1970–78.

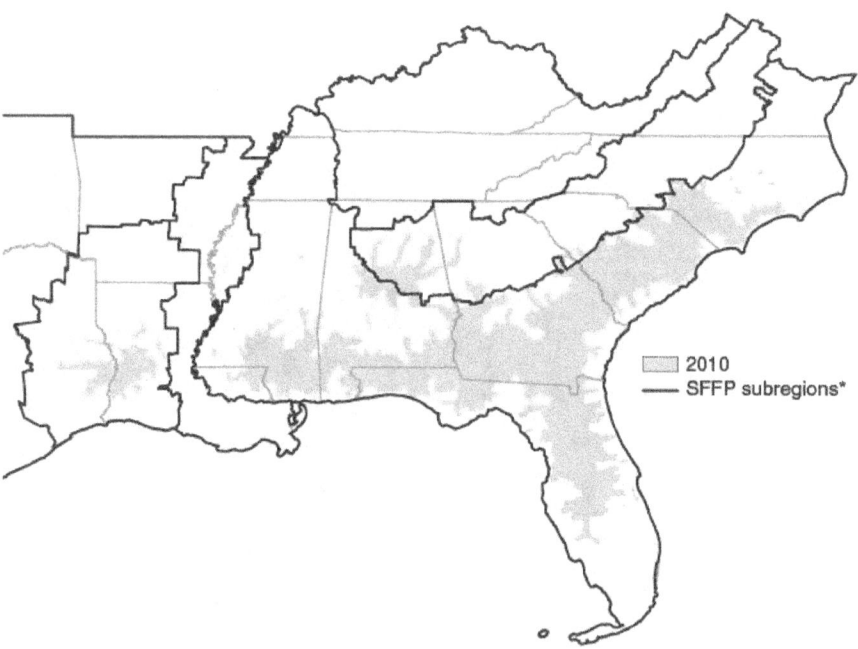

2010
— SFFP subregions*

* Southern Forests Futures Project delineations (Wear and others 2009).

Figure 5—Geographic extent of longleaf pine in the South as sampled by the Forest Inventory and Analysis program, 2010.

Table 2—Area of all forest land within each forest-type group by subregion, 2010

| Forest-type group | Total | Subregion | | | | | |
		Appalachian-Cumberland	Coastal plain (east)	Coastal plain (west)	Midsouth	Mississippi Alluvial Valley	Piedmont
				acres			
White-red-jack pine	497,300	442,416	3,067	0	0	0	51,817
Spruce-fir	29,506	29,506	0	0	0	0	0
Longleaf-slash pine							
Longleaf pine	3,300,717	0	2,938,157	258,872	0	0	103,688
Slash pine	9,915,283	0	9,204,172	703,632	6,065	0	1,415
Loblolly-shortleaf pine	55,857,335	1,318,526	28,618,105	12,079,298	3,130,471	630,523	10,080,413
Other eastern softwood	1,888,150	555,702	167,665	19,491	1,051,937	15,363	77,993
Oak-pine							
Longleaf pine-oak	984,637	0	857,401	39,357	0	0	87,879
All others	21,569,389	2,470,857	9,483,959	3,162,600	2,191,970	117,505	4,142,497
Oak-hickory	81,500,242	27,250,265	20,137,118	4,983,012	13,779,799	947,874	14,402,175
Oak-gum-cypress	23,631,606	268,686	15,711,146	3,324,936	658,189	3,059,516	609,133
Elm-ash-cottonwood	9,965,585	1,073,456	3,069,227	736,947	2,118,644	1,953,142	1,014,168
Maple-beech-birch	1,895,897	1,870,861	25,036	0	0	0	0
Ash-birch	11,797	10,160	0	0	0	0	1,638
Other hardwood	902,603	254,659	91,033	23,866	478,551	19,081	35,414
Tropical hardwood	720,067	0	720,067	0	0	0	0
Exotic hardwood	934,083	95,973	251,699	383,550	75,784	73,480	53,597
Nonstocked	2,723,166	116,281	1,545,834	264,648	376,788	222,388	197,227
Total	216,327,364	35,757,348	92,823,686	25,980,207	23,868,198	7,038,873	30,859,052

(table 3). Currently southern forests are dominated by oak-hickory forest types that cover an estimated 81.5 million acres or 38 percent of southern forest land. The longleaf pine/oak forest type accounts for an estimated 984,000 acres across the South, or about 0.5 percent of southern forest land.

The current estimate of 3.3 million acres of the longleaf pine forest type represents a decline of nearly 88 million acres from historical estimates of longleaf pine forest coverage in the Southern United States. About 3 percent of the original longleaf pine forests found in the Southern United States currently remain. The vast majority, about 89 percent, or 2.9 million acres of the total longleaf pine forest type occurs in the East Coastal Plain with large concentrations located in the panhandle of Florida and southern Alabama, Georgia, and Mississippi (fig. 6).

In order to provide a comparison of the current area occupied by longleaf pine forests to the historic coverage of longleaf pine, timberland (forest land available for timber production) area occupied by the longleaf pine forest type was estimated for each decade beginning with the 1970s. Absolute and relative change in timberland area occupied by the longleaf pine forest type was calculated for each

county in the South by comparing the 1970s estimate to the estimate for 2010. The largest absolute changes in longleaf pine forest-type timberland area occurred in western Louisiana and along the coast in Mississippi, Alabama, and Florida, along with portions of North Carolina (fig. 7). Gains within the longleaf pine type from 1970 to 2010 were experienced throughout the South. The largest concentrations of counties with estimated gains were located along the fall-line between the Piedmont and the East Coastal Plain. Relative to the area the longleaf pine type occupied in 1970, the most concentrated severe losses occurred in the Atlantic region of the East Coastal Plain (fig. 8). Two hundred fifty-five counties are estimated to have had timberland area identified as belonging to the longleaf pine type in either 1970, in 2010, or in both 1970 and 2010. Greater than 70 percent losses occurred in a total of 89 counties (32 percent of counties) while a 100-percent loss of longleaf pine forests was estimated in 62 counties (23 percent of counties) across the South. About 30 percent (84 counties) experienced some gain in longleaf pine forest-type acreage over the same period. A similar analysis of the longleaf pine/oak forest type indicated gains in the Southeastern United States while losses were concentrated in the West Coastal Plain and the gulf coast of Alabama and Mississippi (fig. 9).

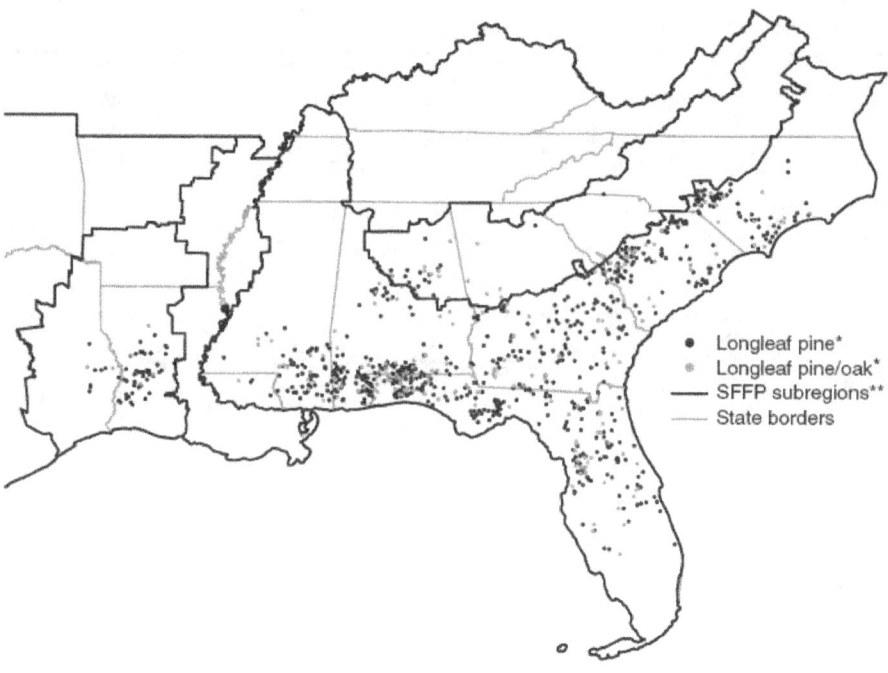

* Plot locations are approximate.
** Southern Forests Futures Project delineations (Wear and others 2009).

Figure 6—Approximate location of the longleaf pine and longleaf pine/oak forest types as sampled by the Southern Research Station Forest Inventory and Analysis unit, 2010.

Table 3—Percent of forest land classified as longleaf pine forest type by subregion, 2010

| Subregion | Forest type | | |
	Longleaf pine	Longleaf pine/oak	Total
	percent		
Appalachian, Cumberland	0.00	0.00	0.00
Coastal plain, (east)	3.17	0.92	4.09
Coastal plain, (west)	1.00	0.15	1.15
Midsouth	0.00	0.00	0.00
Mississippi Alluvial Valley	0.00	0.00	0.00
Piedmont	0.34	0.28	0.62
Total	1.53	0.46	1.98

0.0 = no sample for the cell or a value of >0.0 but <0.05.

Recent Changes in Longleaf Pine Extent

Forest communities are dynamic. As time elapses, management regimes change, and natural and anthropogenic disturbances occur on the landscape. Forests are altered to reflect both autogenic and allogenic forces. To better understand the changes occurring in longleaf pine dominated forests in the South, we compared the current and previous forest-type classification for remeasured plots designated as longleaf pine forest type in either the current or the previous inventory. Results indicate that the largest percentage of longleaf pine acreage is being lost to the loblolly pine (5.60 percent) and longleaf pine/oak (5.32 percent) forest types (table 4). About 56 percent of the acreage lost to the loblolly pine forest type is a result of a change to planted loblolly pine. This suggests that losses to planted loblolly pine account for a considerable proportion of the overall loss of longleaf pine acreage to other forest types. Losses to the mixed longleaf pine/oak forest type suggests encroachment of hardwood stems within a longleaf pine stand possibly due to the lack of fire in the system.

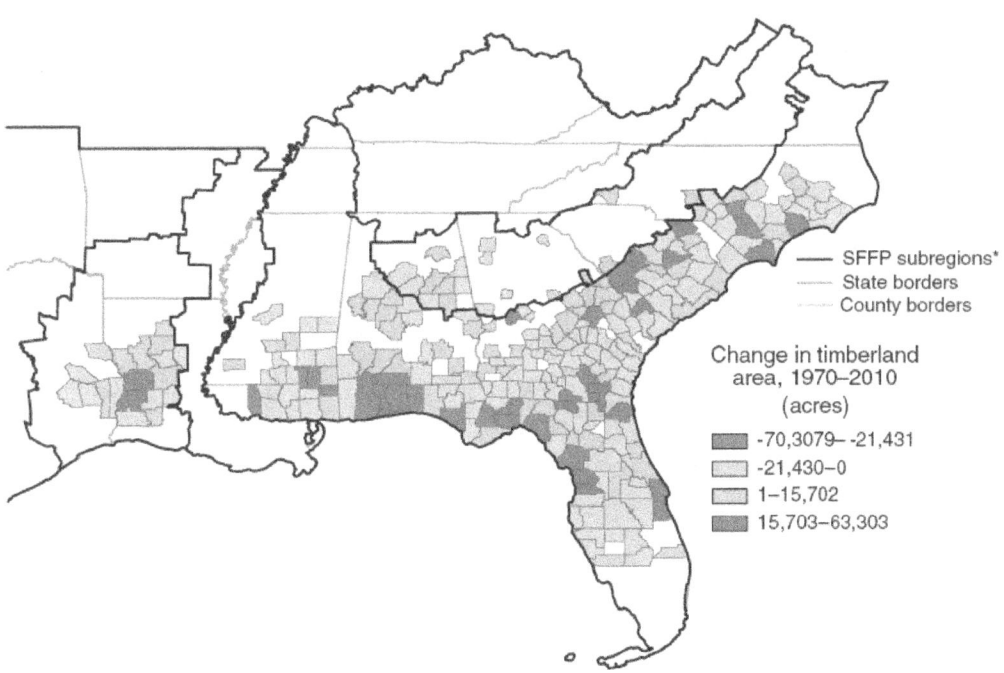

Change in timberland
area, 1970–2010
(acres)

- ■ -70,3079--21,431
- □ -21,430-0
- □ 1-15,702
- ■ 15,703-63,303

—— SFFP subregions*
—— State borders
—— County borders

* Southern Forests Futures Project delineations (Wear and others 2009).

Figure 7—Absolute change in area of timberland occupied by the longleaf pine forest type, 1970–2010.

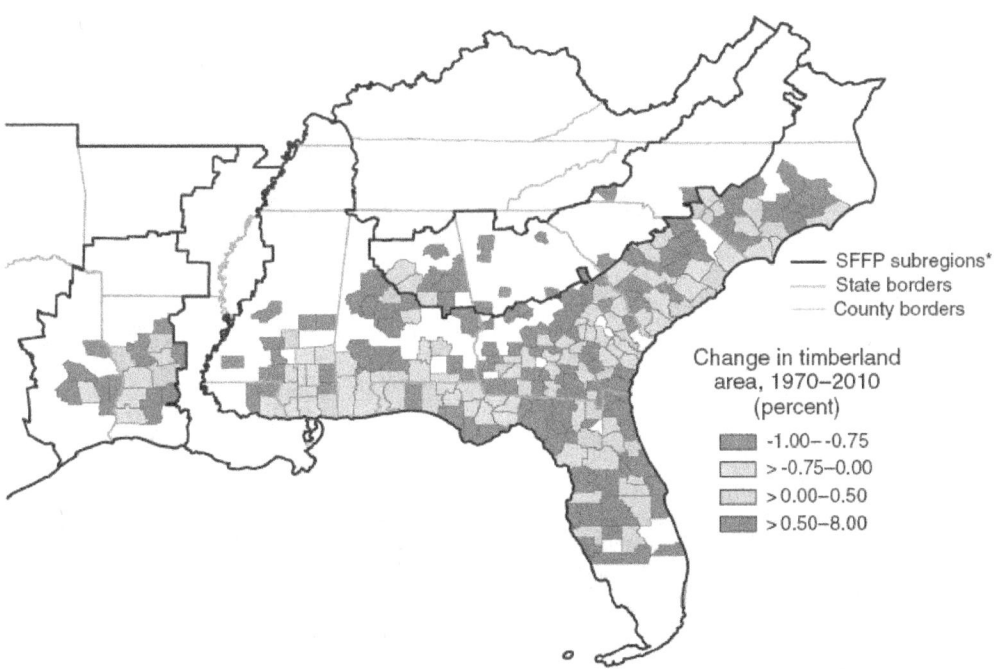

Change in timberland
area, 1970–2010
(percent)

- ■ -1.00--0.75
- □ > -0.75-0.00
- □ > 0.00-0.50
- ■ > 0.50-8.00

—— SFFP subregions*
—— State borders
—— County borders

* Southern Forests Futures Project delineations (Wear and others 2009).

Figure 8—Relative change in area of timberland occupied by the longleaf pine forest type, 1970–2010.

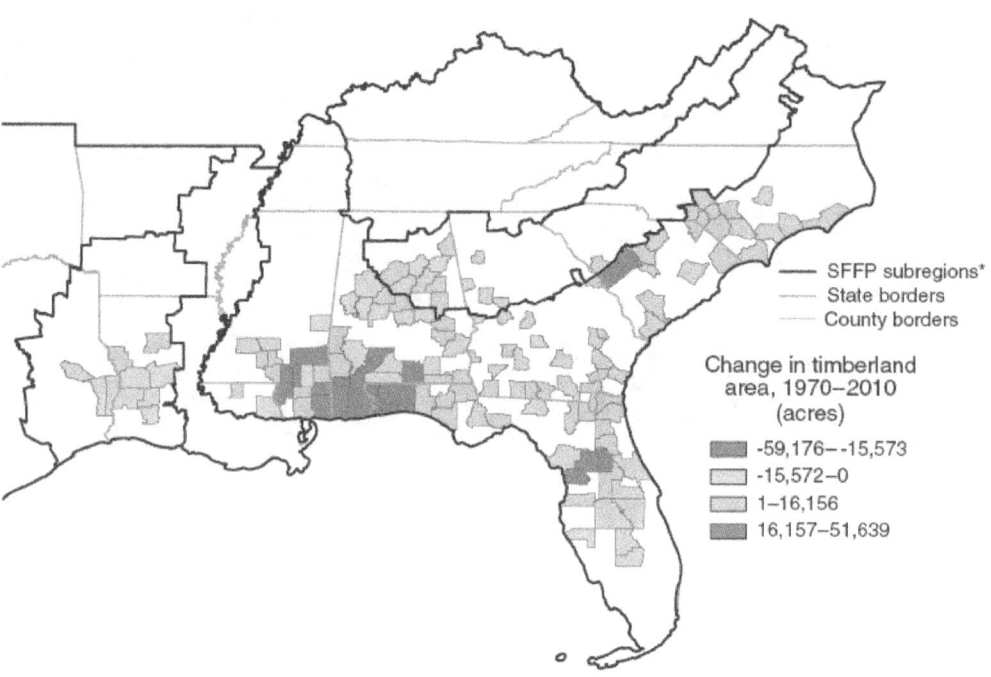

* Southern Forests Futures Project delineations (Wear and others 2009).

Figure 9—Absolute change in area of timberland occupied by the longleaf pine/oak forest type, 1970–2010.

While some longleaf pine acreage is being lost to other forest types, gains are occurring as well. The largest gains (10.32 percent) in longleaf pine acreage are a result of changes within stands classified as longleaf pine/oak during the previous inventory (table 4). In addition, some gains (3.20 percent) in longleaf pine forest acreage are being realized from changes to previously classified loblolly pine stands.

Characteristics of Remaining Longleaf Pine

Sixty-two percent of the existing longleaf pine dominated forests are owned by nonindustrial private landowners and the remaining 38 percent by public land management agencies (table 5). Although public lands only constitute about 10 percent of all forest land in this region, they support a larger percentage of the area in longleaf pine. Ownership stability over the long term and public agency ecosystem management programs that do not exclusively emphasize commodity production provide a more secure environment for this long-lived tree species that can be sustained by less intensive management practices. Public lands more often exist as larger, less fragmented tracts with linkages that provide ecological connections among otherwise isolated longleaf pine forest "islands." The many

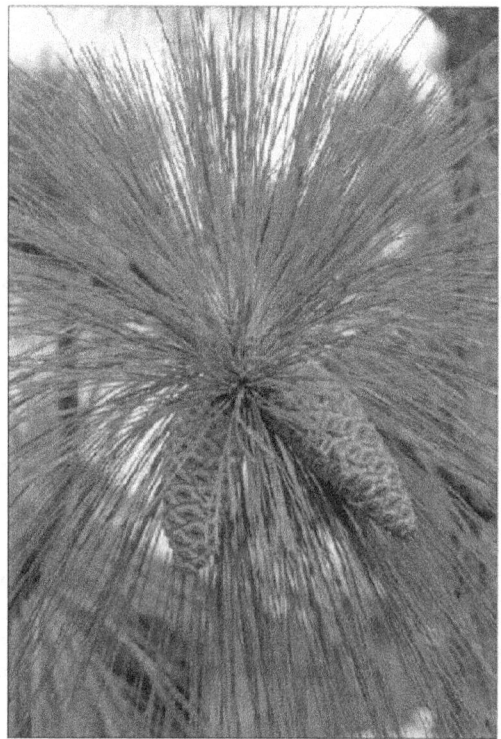

Foliage and cones of longleaf pine (*Pinus palustris*). (photo by Erich G. Vallery, U.S. Forest Service)

Table 4—Estimate of losses and gains to the longleaf pine forest type as compared to previous inventories, 2010

Forest type	Losses[a]	Gains[b]
	percent	
Slash pine	2.26	1.05
Loblolly pine	5.60	3.20
Shortleaf pine	0.38	—
Pond pine	0.51	0.02
Longleaf pine/oak	5.32	10.32
Virginia pine/southern red oak	0.04	—
Loblolly pine	0.71	1.26
Slash pine	—	0.31
Other pine	—	0.01
Post oak/blackjack oak	0.00	—
White oak/red oak/hickory	—	0.71
Northern red oak	—	0.09
Sassafras/persimmon	0.59	0.43
Sweetgum/yellow-poplar	—	0.95
Scrub oak	0.45	0.13
Cherry/white ash/yellow-poplar	0.38	0.18
Red maple/oak	0.10	0.18
Mixed upland hardwoods	1.82	1.56
Sweetgum/nuttall oak/willow oak	—	0.01
Bald cypress/water tupelo	—	0.01
Sweetbay/swamp tupelo/red maple	0.12	0.01
Unknown	0.19	1.12
No designation	1.81	8.32

— = negligible.

[a] Percent of longleaf pine acreage of previous inventory lost to each forest type.

[b] Percent of longleaf pine acreage of current inventory gained from each forest type.

resource values and desirable ecological attributes of longleaf pine forests also complement the land management mission of most public agencies.

The longleaf pine/oak forest type was slightly more heavily concentrated on private land. About 70 percent of all acreage of the longleaf pine/oak type was in private hands while an estimated 60 percent of the longleaf pine forest-type acreage is privately owned. The ownership patterns of the West Coastal Plain differed from the others in that 48 and 40 percent of the longleaf pine and longleaf pine/oak acreage, respectively, were privately held (table 5). The ownership pattern of the East Coastal Plain and the Piedmont matched that of the regionwide averages.

Many public land agencies such as the U.S. Department of Agriculture Forest Service National Forest System, the Department of Defense, and the U.S. Fish and Wildlife have dedicated considerable resources to inventorying and monitoring the longleaf pine resources located within their respective boundaries. Excellent fine-scale (stand) data exist within these land management agencies. Readers should be cautious when comparing stand-level data from public land agencies with sample estimates provided here by FIA. Estimates provided by FIA are based on sampling a systematic grid across the United States with plots representing a total of about 6,000 acres. Often, fine-scale data collected by public land management agencies can represent a true inventory or multiple resource plots within a given stand. While the broadscale inventory estimates provided by FIA may not match precisely with fine-scale information, the estimates derived from fine-scale data collection should fall with the bounds of the sampling error associated with the broadscale FIA estimate. Readers should use each estimate to answer resource questions at the scale that matches the scale of data collection.

Combined, the longleaf pine and longleaf pine/oak forest types are primarily represented by stands with an age of ≤50 years (table 6). Fifty-nine percent of all stands are in age classes of ≤41 to 50 years. On the other hand, only 18 percent of all longleaf pine dominated forests are in stands with ages between 0 to 10 years (fig. 10a). Viewed separately, both the longleaf pine and longleaf pine/oak forest types have similar age class distributions with the longleaf pine/oak forest type having about one-third of the area of the longleaf pine forest type in most age classes.

Fifty-eight percent of the longleaf pine forest-type acres support stands ≤50 years old (fig. 10b). Stands older than 80 years makeup just 7 percent of the longleaf pine acreage (table 6). None of the stands in the West Coastal Plain are older than 90 years. The longleaf pine forests in the East Coastal Plain and the Piedmont both exhibit a bimodal-age class structure with peaks in the 61–70-year age class and the 0–10-year age class. Similarly, the longleaf pine/oak forest type exhibits a peak in the 0–10-year age class (fig. 10c). While only a small proportion of longleaf pine dominated forests are within the older age classes, a bimodal distribution indicates that younger cohorts are developing. These younger cohorts are valuable for the long-term sustainability of the species and ecosystem. One difference may be the somewhat disjunct population of longleaf pine dominated forests in the West Coastal Plain. The area of the longleaf pine forest type in this region exhibits a peak in the 41–50-year age class. Unlike the longleaf pine type of the East Coastal Plain and the Piedmont, this type in the West Coastal Plain does not appear to be developing a younger cohort (0–10- and 11–20-year age classes). While not alarming, this does warrant further investigation and could be indicative of issues such as limited planting or inadequate regeneration. Additionally,

Table 5—Area of forest land by longleaf pine forest type, region, and ownership class, 2010

Forest type and region	All ownership	Ownership class						
		U.S. Forest Service	U.S. Fish and Wildlife Service	Department of Defense	Other Federal	State	County and municipal	Private
				thousand acres				
Longleaf								
Coastal plain (east)	2,938,157.47	453,374.34	53,395.47	254,127.26	53,694.76	329,051.18	28,542.17	1,765,972.29
Coastal plain (west)	258,872.30	116,927.80	0.00	10,662.13	0.00	0.00	6,092.65	125,189.73
Piedmont	103,687.66	23,689.08	0.00	0.00	0.00	6,090.85	0.00	73,907.73
Total	3,300,717.43	593,991.22	53,395.47	264,789.39	53,694.76	335,142.03	34,634.81	1,965,069.75
Longleaf-oak								
Coastal plain (east)	857,401.14	61,905.71	6,522.80	45,484.02	19,106.23	109,091.63	4,691.47	610,599.28
Coastal plain (west)	39,357.08	17,482.63	0.00	6,092.65	0.00	0.00	0.00	15,781.81
Piedmont	87,878.57	13,167.20	0.00	0.00	0.00	11,313.29	0.00	63,398.08
Total	984,636.79	92,555.54	6,522.80	51,576.67	19,106.23	120,404.92	4,691.47	689,779.17
Combined longleaf								
Coastal plain (east)	3,795,558.61	515,280.05	59,918.27	299,611.28	72,800.98	438,142.81	33,233.64	2,376,571.58
Coastal plain (west)	298,229.38	134,410.43	0.00	16,754.78	0.00	0.00	6,092.65	140,971.54
Piedmont	191,566.23	36,856.28	0.00	0.00	0.00	17,404.14	0.00	137,305.81
Total	4,285,354.23	686,546.76	59,918.27	316,366.05	72,800.98	455,546.95	39,326.28	2,654,848.93

Numbers in rows and columns may not sum to totals due to rounding.
0.0 = no sample for the cell or a value of >0.0 but <0.05.

Table 6—Area of forest land by longleaf forest type, region, and stand-age class, 2010

Forest type and region	All classes	Stand-age class (*years*)										
		0–10	11–20	21–30	31–40	41–50	51–60	61–70	71–80	81–90	91–100	100+
						acres						
Longleaf pine												
Coastal plain (east)	2,938,157	523,467	331,929	277,135	316,814	296,992	314,262	343,312	331,588	140,302	50,605	11,752
Coastal plain (west)	258,872	18,359	7,024	32,764	0	65,756	52,962	54,158	21,974	5,875	0	0
Piedmont	103,688	37,581	3,164	6,091	6,383	6,091	10,659	16,969	6,091	6,091	0	4,568
Total	3,300,717	579,406	342,117	315,989	323,197	368,839	377,883	414,438	359,653	152,269	50,605	16,320
Longleaf pine/oak												
Coastal plain (east)	857,401	138,426	71,085	83,453	98,414	110,924	133,128	134,892	45,551	29,878	11,650	0
Coastal plain (west)	39,357	18,015	0	0	0	9,773	11,569	0	0	0	0	0
Piedmont	87,879	22,616	1,523	6,083	1,166	21,913	5,554	12,182	12,274	4,568	0	0
Total	984,637	179,058	72,608	89,536	99,580	142,610	150,250	147,074	57,825	34,446	11,650	0
Combined longleaf												
Coastal plain (east)	3,795,559	661,893	403,014	360,588	415,228	407,916	447,390	478,204	377,139	170,181	62,255	11,752
Coastal plain (west)	298,229	36,373	7,024	32,764	0	75,529	64,531	54,158	21,974	5,875	0	0
Piedmont	191,566	60,197	4,687	12,174	7,549	28,004	16,213	29,151	18,365	10,659	0	4,568
Total	4,285,354	758,463	414,726	405,525	422,777	511,449	528,133	561,512	417,478	186,715	62,255	16,320

Numbers in rows and columns may not sum to totals due to rounding.

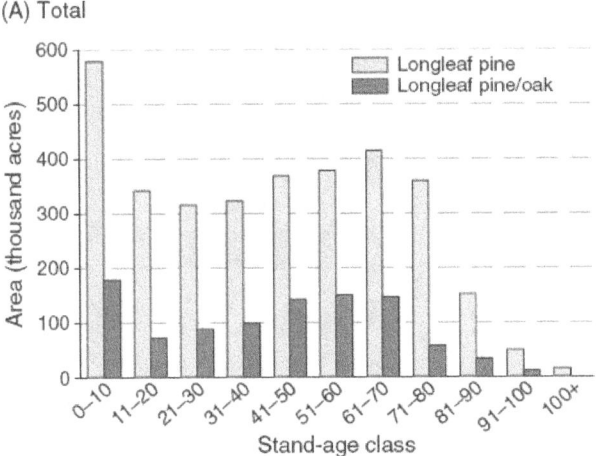

(A) Total

Longleaf pine
Longleaf pine/oak

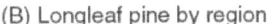

(B) Longleaf pine by region

Coastal Plain (east)
Coastal Plain (west)
Piedmont

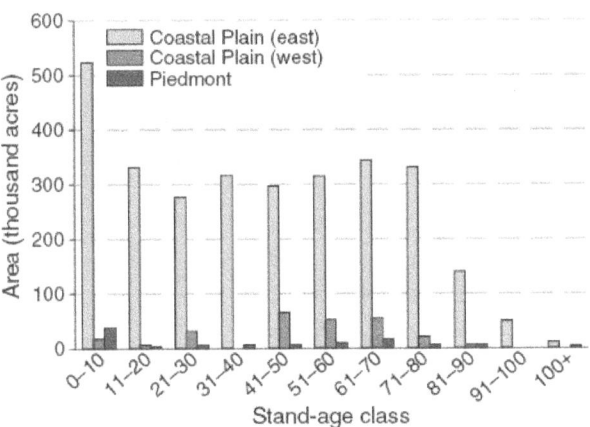

(C) Longleaf pine/oak by region

Coastal Plain (east)
Coastal Plain (west)
Piedmont

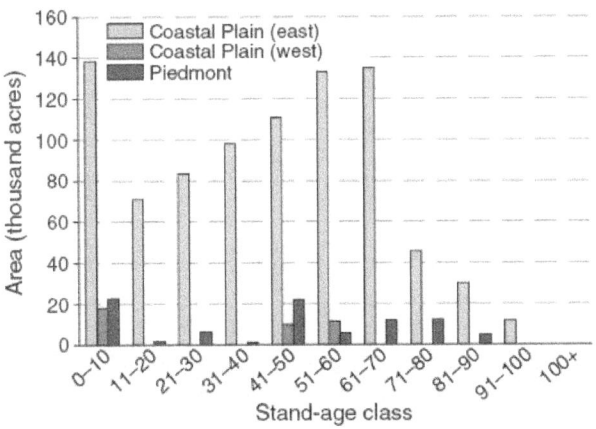

Figure 10—Area of longleaf pine and longleaf pine/oak forest types on forest land by stand-age class (A) Total, (B) Longleaf pine by region, and (C) Longleaf pine/oak by region, 2010.

FIA stand-age estimation procedures are biased toward representation of stand age as if all stands were of an even-aged structure. FIA procedures provides the age of the larger overstory trees within the stand. Longleaf pine is not locked into the even-aged model and in fact is often found in multiaged stands. Therefore, some of the stands sampled in the older age classes potentially have adequate advance regeneration due the complex uneven-aged structure common in longleaf pine dominated systems across the South.

Across the South, an estimated 1.1 million acres (27 percent) of longleaf pine and longleaf pine/oak forest types have been planted. An estimated 2.3 million acres (71 percent) of all longleaf pine dominated forests originated from natural regeneration (fig. 11). Some 967,000 acres of the longleaf pine forest type have been planted throughout the South. While some of the planted acreage was first established primarily with another species of pine, the vast majority (92 percent) was planted primarily with longleaf pine (table 7). An estimated 869,000 acres have been planted in the East Coastal Plain that are now classified as the longleaf pine forest type. Planted longleaf pine forest-type acreage represents a roughly similar proportion (28, 27, and 30 percent in the Piedmont, West, and East Coastal Plains, respectively) in each of the three regions in the South where longleaf pine forests are currently found. Similarly, planted longleaf pine that is classified as longleaf pine/oak is similar across the South. Planted longleaf pine dominated forests (longleaf pine and longleaf pine/oak forest types) comprise the largest proportion of the younger stands (fig. 12). In fact, of the 1.1 million acres of planted longleaf pine dominated forests, about 84 percent were ≤25 years old, while only 13 percent of natural stands were ≤25 years old.

The greatest concentrations of longleaf pine trees are located in the East Coastal Plain, particularly in the panhandle of Florida and southern Alabama and Mississippi (fig. 13). Additional concentrations exist near the border with the Piedmont region in central South Carolina. Interestingly, while the total number of planted longleaf pine trees (fig. 14) exhibits a similar spatial pattern of concentration as all longleaf pine trees (fig. 13), when planted longleaf pine is displayed as a percentage of all longleaf pine trees within a given county, the spatial pattern of concentration appears to reflect the opposite (fig. 15). This may suggest that in areas where longleaf pine is limited it is more heavily represented by planted trees.

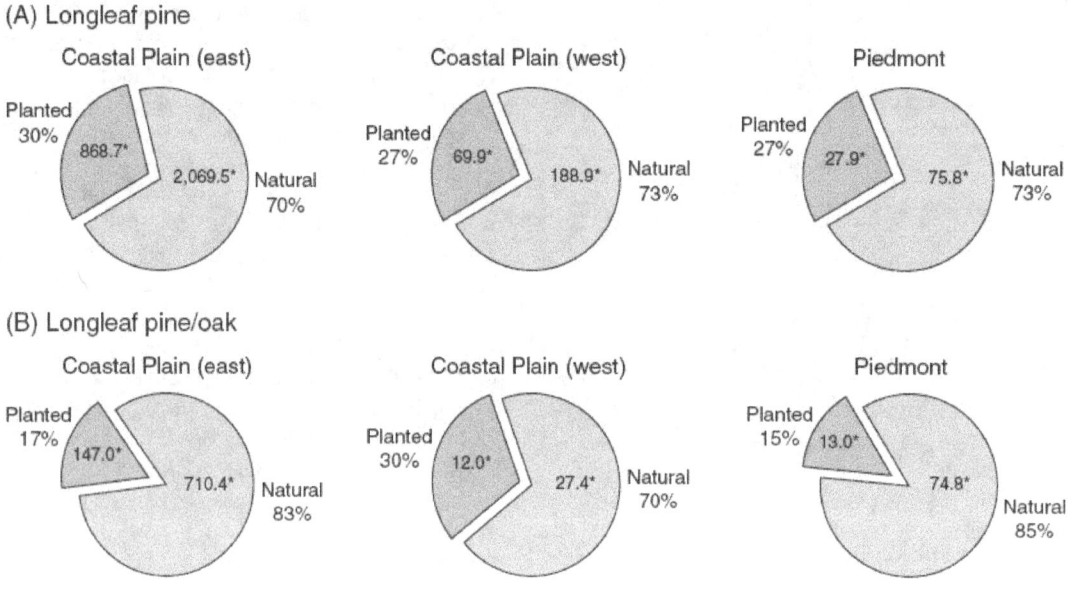

(A) Longleaf pine

Coastal Plain (east)

Planted 30% 868.7* Natural 70% 2,069.5*

Coastal Plain (west)

Planted 27% 69.9* Natural 73% 188.9*

Piedmont

Planted 27% 27.9* Natural 73% 75.8*

(B) Longleaf pine/oak

Coastal Plain (east)

Planted 17% 147.0* Natural 83% 710.4*

Coastal Plain (west)

Planted 30% 12.0* Natural 70% 27.4*

Piedmont

Planted 15% 13.0* Natural 85% 74.8*

* Thousand acres.

Figure 11—Area of forest land classified as (A) Longleaf pine and (B) Longleaf pine/oak forest types by region and stand origin, 2010.

Table 7—Area of planted longleaf pine forest type by primary planted tree species, 2010

Forest type	Planted tree species		All forests
	Longleaf pine	Longleaf pine-oak	
	thousand acres		
Slash pine	49.9	10.3	60.2
Longleaf pine	882.2	159.5	1,041.7
Loblolly pine	14.1	0.0	14.1
Papershell pinyon pine	1.5	0.0	1.5
No species listed	18.8	2.2	21.0

0.0 = no sample for the cell or a value of >0.0 but <0.05.

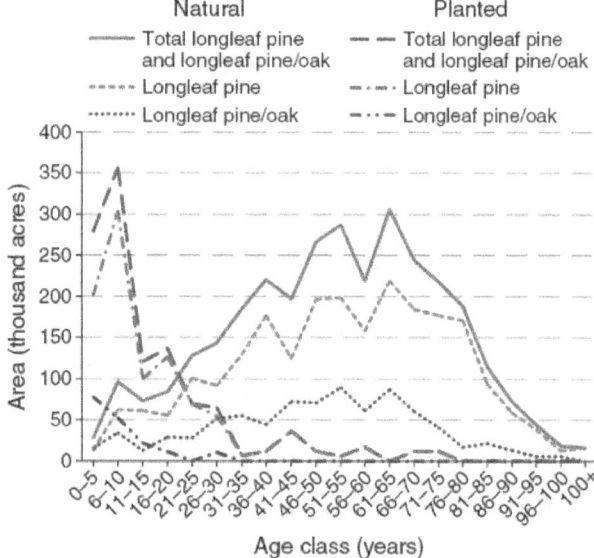

Figure 12—Area of forest land by 5-year age class and stand origin for longleaf pine and longleaf pine/oak forest types, southern region, 2010.

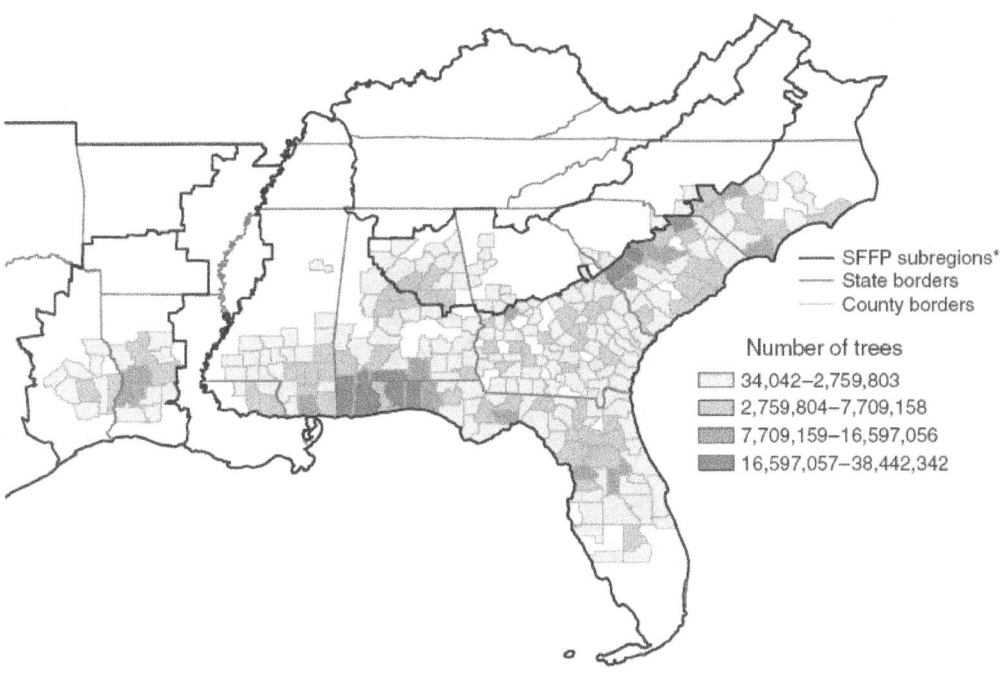

* Southern Forests Futures Project delineations (Wear and others 2009).

Figure 13—Estimated number of longleaf pine trees on forest land by county, 2010.

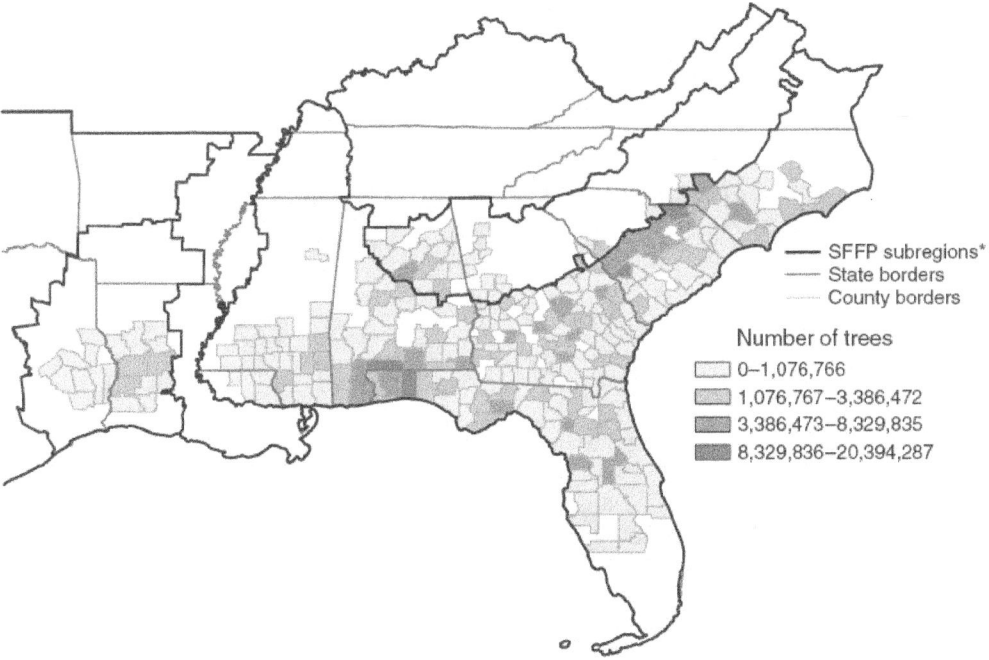

* Southern Forests Futures Project delineations (Wear and others 2009).

Figure 14—Estimated number of longleaf pine trees located within stands of planted origin, 2010.

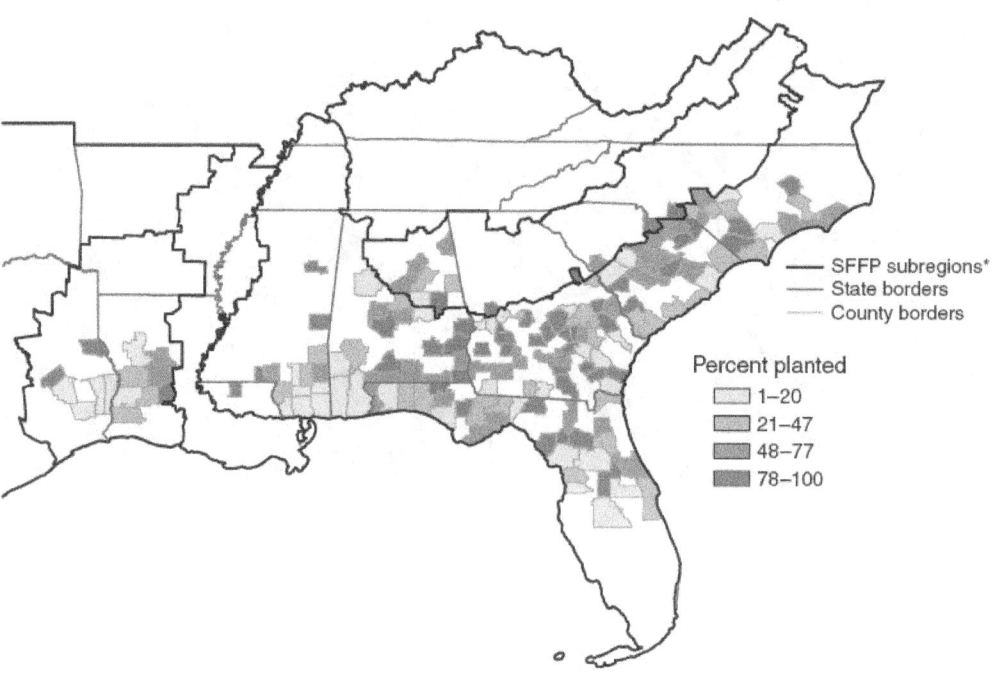

* Southern Forests Futures Project delineations (Wear and others 2009).

Figure 15—Percent of total longleaf pine trees within stands of planted origin, 2010. (Note: longleaf pine stems may occur as volunteers in stands planted with other species.)

Stand-size class is often used as an indication of the developmental stage of a particular stand or forest. These classes are broken into large-, medium-, and small-diameter classes. The large-diameter class contains all trees ≥9 inches in diameter. The medium-diameter class contains trees 5–8.9 inches and the small-diameter class contains trees <5 inches in diameter. In 2010, 49 percent of longleaf pine dominated forest land acreage was classified as large diameter according to FIA stand-size class definitions (fig. 16, table 8). While many of the longleaf pine/oak stands are classified as small-diameter stands, those stands have a large proportion of small hardwood stems (fig. 17) that contribute to the stand-size classification. The existing mixed longleaf pine/oak stands may be primarily longleaf pine stands with an abundance of hardwood stems occupying the midstory. These stands may represent stands that could easily be restored to a functioning longleaf pine system with minimal management intervention. Counties with the largest area of longleaf pine forests were heavily concentrated in southern Alabama and the panhandle of Florida where Eglin Air Force Base is located (fig. 18). The spatial distribution of longleaf pine forests differed

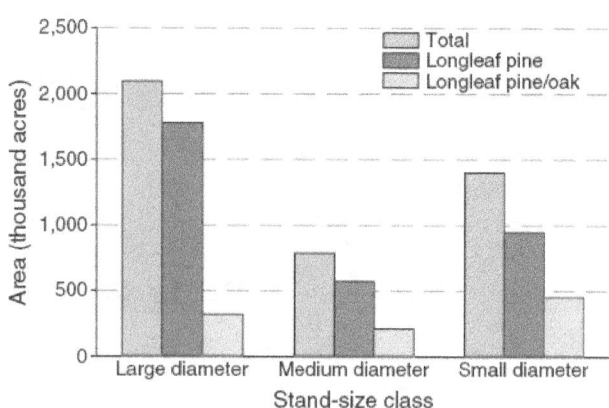

Figure 16—Area of forest land classified as the longleaf forest type by stand-size class, 2010.

Table 8—Area of forest land classified as longleaf pine and longleaf pine/oak forest types by State and stand-size class, 2010

State	Stand-size class		
	Large	Medium	Small
	percent		
Alabama	48	18	34
Florida	48	21	31
Georgia	41	14	45
Louisiana	71	12	17
Mississippi	66	14	20
North Carolina	51	26	23
South Carolina	42	22	36
East Texas	62	0	38
Total	49	18	33

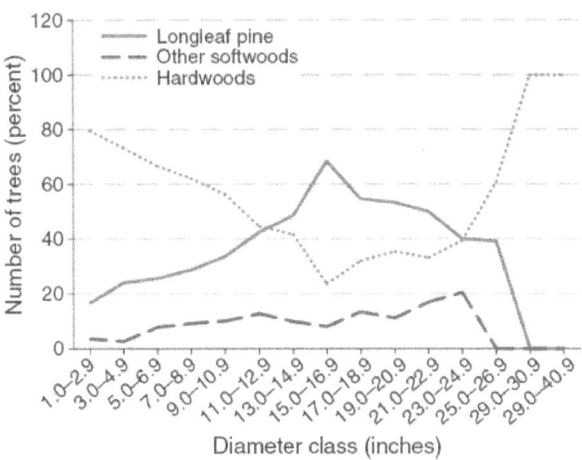

Figure 17—Number of longleaf pine, other softwood, and hardwood trees in stands classified as longleaf pine/oak forest type, 2010.

slightly among each stand-size class collected by the FIA program. Small-diameter longleaf pine forests were heavily concentrated in southern Alabama and the panhandle of Florida (fig. 19). Concentrations of medium-diameter forests were more widely distributed across the longleaf pine range and included areas in central Florida, Florida's panhandle, southern Alabama, south-central South Carolina, and portions of coastal North Carolina (fig. 20). Counties with large areas of longleaf pine forests comprised mostly of large-diameter stems were located in southern Alabama, the panhandle of Florida, western Louisiana, and east Texas

(fig. 21). Using stand-size class as a proxy for developmental stage (Trani and others 2001, Franzreb and others 2011), the implication is that there appears to be a dearth of early successional longleaf pine dominated forests across the South, with the exception of in southern Alabama and the panhandle of Florida. The stand-size class distribution of Western Coastal Plain is particularly concerning due to the uniqueness of the longleaf pine forests in the area (Outcalt 1997). Very few early- and mid-successional longleaf pine forests exist in Louisiana (table 8) where most stands are much further along in development.

Pinus palustris regeneration, Wambaw Ranger District, Francis Marion National Forest, North Carolina. (photo by Bill Lea)

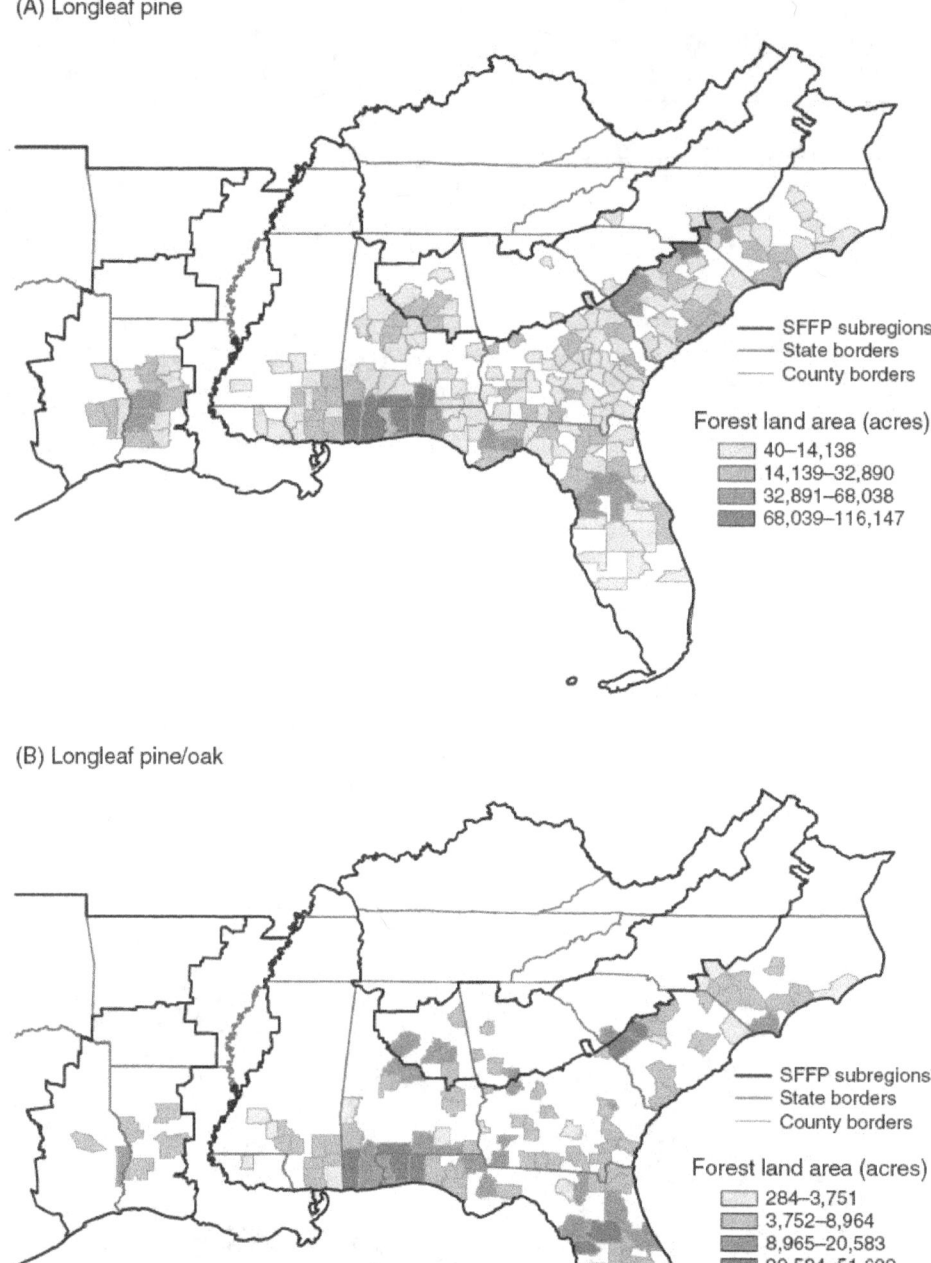

(A) Longleaf pine

SFFP subregions*
State borders
County borders

Forest land area (acres)
40–14,138
14,139–32,890
32,891–68,038
68,039–116,147

(B) Longleaf pine/oak

SFFP subregions*
State borders
County borders

Forest land area (acres)
284–3,751
3,752–8,964
8,965–20,583
20,584–51,639

* Southern Forests Futures Project delineations (Wear and others 2009).

Figure 18—Area of forest land classified as belonging to the (A) Longleaf pine and (B) Longleaf pine/oak forest types by county, 2010.

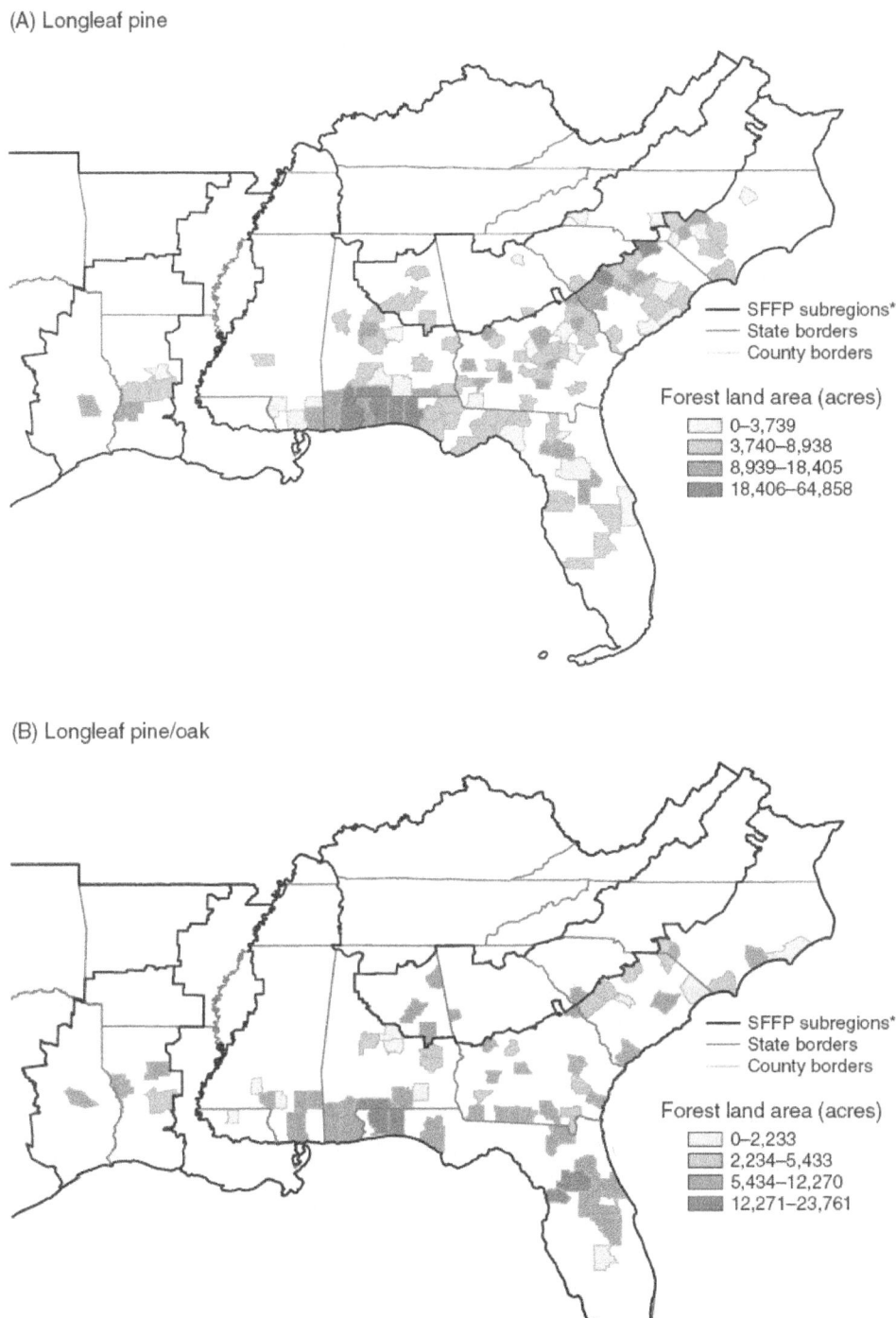

(A) Longleaf pine

SFFP subregions*
State borders
County borders

Forest land area (acres)
- 0–3,739
- 3,740–8,938
- 8,939–18,405
- 18,406–64,858

(B) Longleaf pine/oak

SFFP subregions*
State borders
County borders

Forest land area (acres)
- 0–2,233
- 2,234–5,433
- 5,434–12,270
- 12,271–23,761

* Southern Forests Futures Project delineations (Wear and others 2009).

Figure 19—Area of forest land classified as belonging to the (A) Longleaf pine and (B) Longleaf pine/oak forest types, and small diameter class by county, 2010.

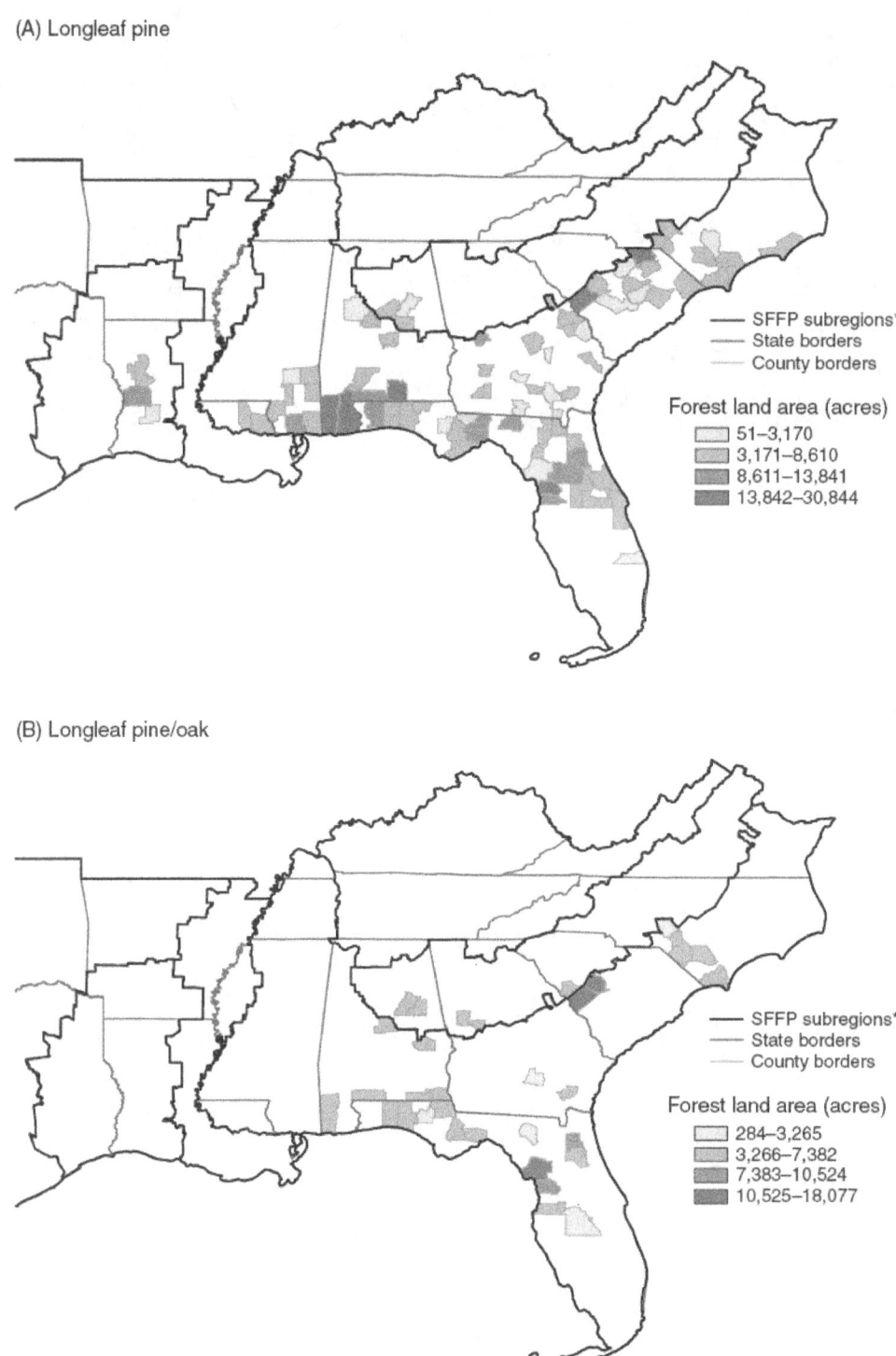

(A) Longleaf pine

SFFP subregions*
State borders
County borders

Forest land area (acres)
51–3,170
3,171–8,610
8,611–13,841
13,842–30,844

(B) Longleaf pine/oak

SFFP subregions*
State borders
County borders

Forest land area (acres)
284–3,265
3,266–7,382
7,383–10,524
10,525–18,077

* Southern Forests Futures Project delineations (Wear and others 2009).

Figure 20—Area of forest land classified as belonging to the (A) Longleaf pine, (B) Longleaf pine/oak forest types, and medium diameter stand-size class by county, 2010.

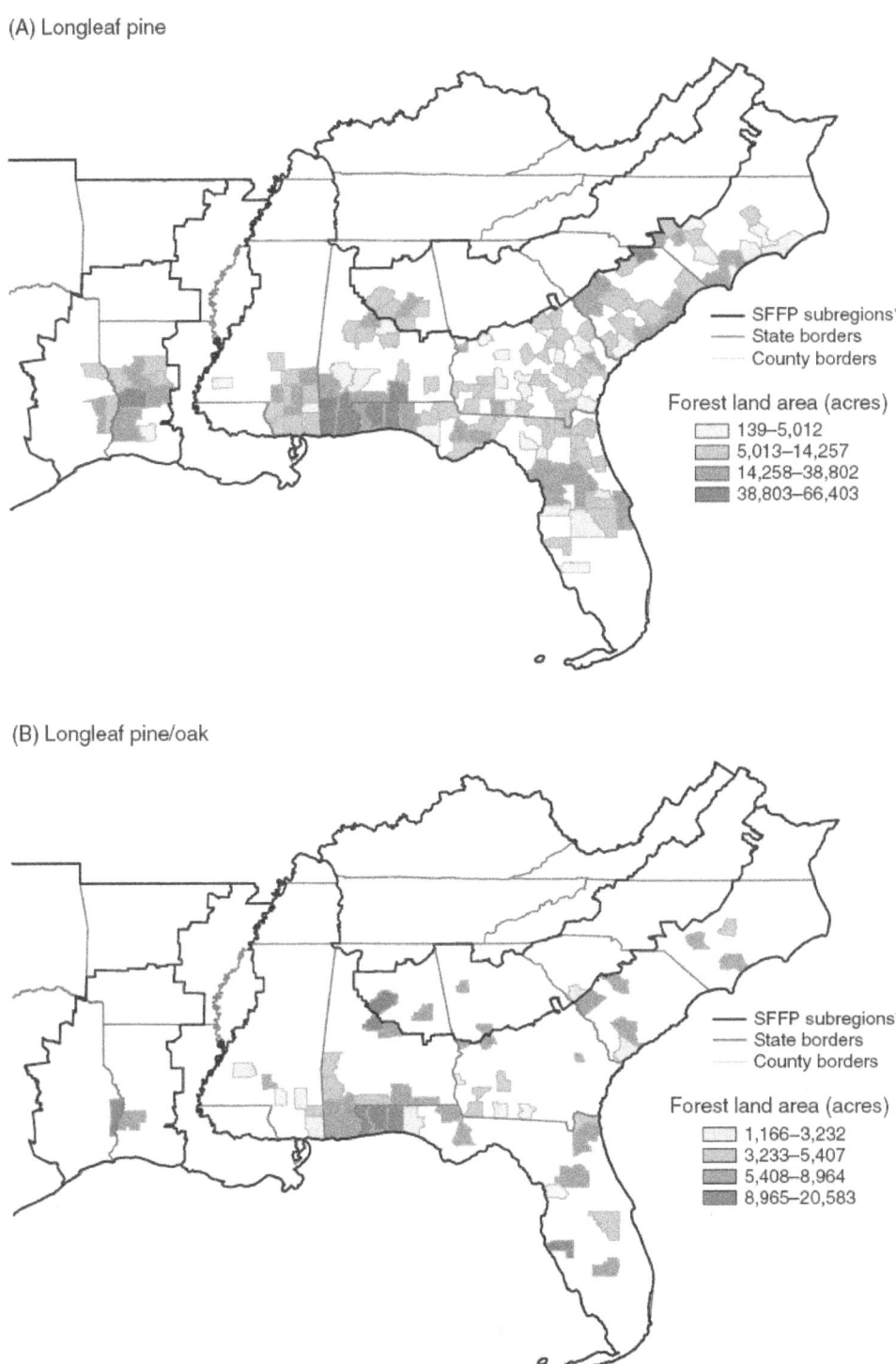

(A) Longleaf pine

SFFP subregions*
State borders
County borders

Forest land area (acres)
139–5,012
5,013–14,257
14,258–38,802
38,803–66,403

(B) Longleaf pine/oak

SFFP subregions*
State borders
County borders

Forest land area (acres)
1,166–3,232
3,233–5,407
5,408–8,964
8,965–20,583

* Southern Forests Futures Project delineations (Wear and others 2009).

Figure 21—Area of forest land classified as belonging to the (A) Longleaf pine, (B) Longleaf pine/oak forest types, and large diameter stand-size class by county, 2010.

Longleaf Pine Population Dynamics

The long-term decline in the population (number of trees) of longleaf pines has been a topic of discussion for many years. Several groups and organizations have worked to ensure this important pine species continues to occupy forests throughout the South. However, longleaf pine trees have vanished from numerous locations over the last approximately 40 years (fig. 22). This suggests that a pattern of long-term population declines may still be occurring. Essentially, FIA is finding longleaf pine in fewer places and on fewer plots.

In order to provide a comparison of current population levels to historic populations of longleaf pine, estimates of live trees on timberland (forest land available for timber production) were compiled for each decade beginning with

the 1970s. For the decades of data compiled, the 1970s had the highest (>1.25 billion) total number of longleaf pine trees (table 9). From that peak, the number of trees fell to a low of just over 795 million trees by the 1990s. Recent estimates show that the population has increased to >910 million trees, yet remains 27 percent below population levels estimated for the 1970s (table 9). The total longleaf pine population on all forest land in the South is estimated to be slightly higher, about 914 million trees in 2010 (table 10). Recent increases appear to be concentrated in the small-diameter classes (table 9) and may be indicative of positive signs for the future of the species.

The majority (77 percent or 705 million trees) of the longleaf pine population is located within forests classified as the longleaf pine-slash pine forest-type group (table 10).

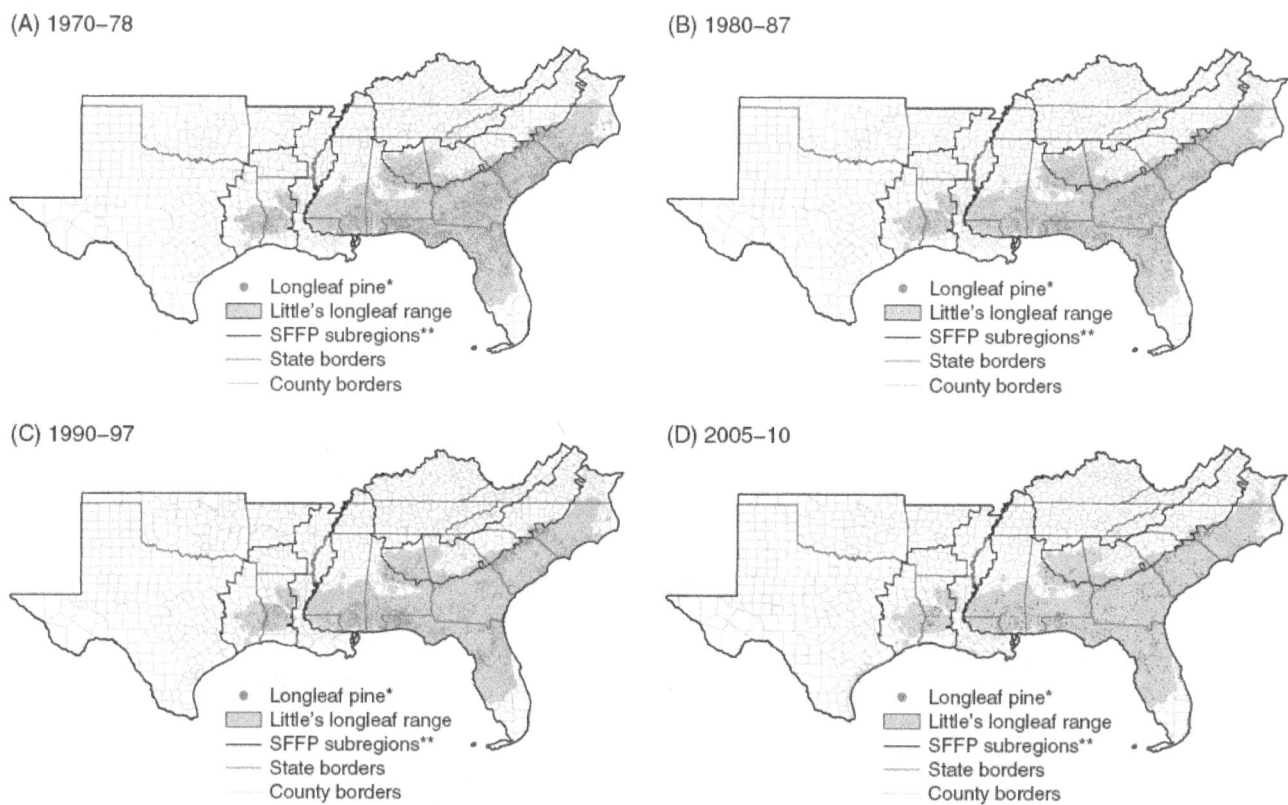

(A) 1970–78

(B) 1980–87

(C) 1990–97

(D) 2005–10

Longleaf pine*
Little's longleaf range
SFFP subregions**
State borders
County borders

* Plot locations are approximate.
** Southern Forests Futures Project delineations (Wear and others 2009).

Figure 22—Approximate location of longleaf pine sampled by the Forest Inventory and Analysis program for (A) 1970–78, (B) 1980–87, (C) 1990–97, and (D) 2005–10 as compared to the documented longleaf pine range (Little 1972).

Table 9—Number of live longleaf pine trees on timberland by year and diameter, 1970–2010

Year	All classes	1.0–2.9	3.0–4.9	5.0–6.9	7.0–8.9	9.0–10.9	11.0–12.9	13.0–14.9	15.0–16.9	17.0–18.9	19.0–20.9	21.0–22.9	23.0–24.9	25.0–26.9	27.0–28.9	29.0–30.9	31.0–32.9
							million trees										
1970	1,250.76	375.81	285.59	185.95	144.51	115.24	81.31	39.69	15.30	5.19	1.60	0.35	0.15	0.04	0.03	0.01	0.00
1980	961.65	281.82	200.55	135.73	108.65	95.75	69.72	40.51	19.05	6.98	1.94	0.59	0.23	0.08	0.03	0.00	0.01
1990	795.27	285.60	166.94	94.34	71.14	61.85	51.49	35.46	18.10	6.65	2.32	0.87	0.36	0.16	0.01	0.00	0.00
2010	910.30	370.53	222.26	106.75	60.96	44.87	39.87	32.49	19.25	8.57	3.24	0.86	0.45	0.18	0.04	0.00	0.00

0.0 = no sample for the cell or a value of >0.0 but <0.05.

Table 10—Number of live longleaf pine trees on forest land by forest-type group and diameter class, 2010

Forest-type group	All classes	1.0–2.9	3.0–4.9	5.0–6.9	7.0–8.9	9.0–10.9	11.0–12.9	13.0–14.9	15.0–16.9	17.0–18.9	19.0–20.9	21.0–22.9	23.0–24.9	25.0–26.9	27.0–28.9
							million trees								
Longleaf-slash pine	704.79	287.25	178.49	81.03	45.19	33.08	31.44	24.75	14.10	6.46	2.32	0.43	0.19	0.04	0.04
Loblolly-shortleaf pine	77.27	28.48	16.91	10.81	6.14	4.55	3.14	3.40	1.88	1.17	0.43	0.18	0.14	0.04	0.00
Oak-pine	102.32	45.50	24.36	9.70	6.86	4.97	3.90	3.06	2.43	0.72	0.43	0.21	0.07	0.10	0.00
Oak hickory	26.57	8.40	3.44	5.13	3.10	2.35	1.45	1.16	0.88	0.37	0.21	0.04	0.04	0.00	0.00
Oak-gum-cypress	1.72	0.43	0.43	0.25	0.11	0.14	0.18	0.07	0.11	0.00	0.00	0.00	0.00	0.00	0.00
Tropical hardwoods	0.15	0.00	0.00	0.11	0.04	0.00	0.00	0.00	0.00	0.00	0.00	0.00	0.00	0.00	0.00
Nonstocked	1.56	0.90	0.00	0.26	0.07	0.11	0.04	0.18	0.00	0.00	0.00	0.00	0.00	0.00	0.00
Total	914.36	370.97	223.62	107.28	61.51	45.19	40.15	32.63	19.39	8.71	3.39	0.86	0.45	0.18	0.04

Numbers in rows and columns may not sum to toals due to rounding.
0.0 = no sample for the cell or a value of >0.0 but <0.05.

The second largest population (an estimated 102 million live trees) is found within forests classified as the oak-pine forest-type group. Not surprisingly, the longleaf pine forest type (a subset of the longleaf pine-slash pine forest-type group) contains the largest population of longleaf pine trees (table 11). Seventy-four percent or an estimated 672 million longleaf pine trees occupy forests classified as the longleaf pine forest type. Other forest types with large populations of longleaf pine trees are the longleaf pine/oak, loblolly pine, slash pine, and southern scrub oak forest-type communities.

Just over 1 percent (9.1 million) longleaf pine trees are lost to mortality annually (table 12). Most (89 percent) of the loss occurred in the East Coastal Plain where annual losses amounted to 8.1 million trees. Trees die for a variety of reasons, but weather is the major cause of death according to latest FIA estimates. Other research has shown that

Table 11—Number of live longleaf pine trees on forest land by forest type for the five forest types with the largest estimated populations of the longleaf pine species, 2010

Forest type	Live longleaf pine trees	
	-- *number* --	*percent*
Longleaf pine	672,458,552	73.5
Longleaf pine/oak	91,027,445	10.0
Loblolly pine	68,246,947	7.5
Slash pine	32,334,892	3.5
Southern scrub oak	11,948,753	1.3

Table 12—Annual mortality on forest land for longleaf pine species by region and diameter class, 2010

Region	All classes	Diameter class (*inches at breast height*)												
		1.0–2.9	3.0–4.9	5.0–6.9	7.0–8.9	9.0–10.9	11.0–12.9	13.0–14.9	15.0–16.9	17.0–18.9	19.0–20.9	21.0–22.9	23.0–24.9	25.0–26.9
		million trees												
Coastal plain (east)	8,145.7	4,449.0	1,859.9	577.2	350.4	249.7	252.7	160.5	157.1	37.5	35.0	5.5	8.8	2.4
Coastal plain (west)	586.9	249.8	187.3	7.7	6.8	23.2	37.0	1.3	32.6	31.7	9.6	0.0	0.0	0.0
Piedmont	369.4	164.8	82.4	47.5	38.5	30.1	6.0	0.0	0.0	0.0	0.0	0.0	0.0	0.0
Total	9,102.0	4,863.6	2,129.6	632.4	395.7	303.0	295.7	161.8	189.7	69.1	44.6	5.5	8.8	2.4

Numbers in rows and columns may not sum to toals due to rounding.

0.0 = no sample for the cell or a value of >0.0 but <0.05.

windthrow from hurricanes and tornadoes have felled large numbers of longleaf pine (Croker 1987, Palik and Pederson 1996, Brockway and others 2005). In addition, lightning has played a role in the mortality of individual longleaf pines and groups of trees (Komarek 1968, Palik and Pederson 1996). Nearly 22 percent of all mortality took place in the 5.0–16.9-inch diameter range, and virtually all of that loss occurred in the East Coastal Plain (table 12). Over three quarters (77 percent) of the annual mortality for longleaf pine appeared in saplings (trees <5 inches in diameter). Only 1.4 percent of all longleaf pine mortality occurred in trees ≥17 inches in diameter.

Productive Capacity of Longleaf Pine

Longleaf pine is an extremely valuable species from both an ecological and economic perspective. Longleaf pine has many unique wood properties and biological characteristics that make it economically competitive with other timber species. For example, longleaf pine grows straighter and produces a stronger wood than the commercially dominant loblolly pine. It is relatively resistant to disease, and is somewhat less susceptible than other southern pine species to mainstem breakage and windthrow from events such as hurricanes that impact the vast majority of the longleaf pine range. As a result, it is important to assess the longleaf pine resource in volumetric terms.

Longleaf pine volume amounted to 4.7 billion cubic feet (table 13), or 2 percent of the 225 billion cubic feet of total volume on timberland across the South. When examining the volume for longleaf pine, the 11.0–16.9-inch diameter range has the greatest portion of the volume attributed to this species. The volume in this range of tree diameters accounts for about 56 percent or 2.6 billion cubic feet of the total volume in longleaf pine species. The 1.0 billion cubic

feet in the 13.0–14.9-inch diameter class is 20 percent of the total volume. Less than 3 percent is in trees >20 inches d.b.h.

Similar to the distribution of longleaf pine acres, the majority of the volume in longleaf pine species is privately owned. Nearly 2.6 billion cubic feet (55 percent) of all the volume of longleaf pine was on privately owned acres. Local, State, and Federal Government ownership accounted for the remaining volume, including 1.1 billion cubic feet of the longleaf pine resource found on U.S. Forest Service lands (table 14). While the majority of the longleaf pine volume is estimated to be within private landholdings, public lands carried greater than average volume per acre of forest land while private lands carried lower than average volume per acre. More than likely, this is an artifact of the differing management strategies employed by the two ownership groups. Additionally, the longleaf pine forests of the West Coastal Plain consistently carried some of the largest volume per-acre estimates with the exception of State owned land in the Piedmont. High per-acre values in the West Coastal Plain are consistent with the stand-size class distribution of the region being skewed to large diameter stands.

Private holdings of longleaf pine forests account for greater acreage in each basal area class (fig. 23). However, like per-acre volume estimates, area estimates within each basal-area class relative to the total area in broad ownership categories (private vs. public) indicate some divergence in management strategies between private and public land owners. A greater proportion of private longleaf pine forest acreage was found to carry per-acre basal area of ≤40 square feet (36 percent) than did public acreage (26 percent). Yet, longleaf pine forest-type stands with >120 square feet per acre were equally rare for both public and private landholdings.

Table 13—All-live volume of longleaf pine species on forest land by region and diameter class, 2010

Region	Diameter class (*inches at breast height*)												Total
	5.0–6.9	7.0–8.9	9.0–10.9	11.0–12.9	13.0–14.9	15.0–16.9	17.0–18.9	19.0–20.9	21.0–22.9	23.0–24.9	25.0–26.9	27.0–28.9	
	cubic feet												
Coastal plain (east)	237,312,089	368,681,853	508,063,395	734,225,906	824,504,153	688,291,449	360,005,675	176,413,216	51,129,272	29,113,000	12,972,174	0	3,990,712,182
Coastal plain (west)	13,596,644	25,028,152	41,584,384	84,185,509	121,690,342	97,822,650	83,004,250	34,775,472	13,467,286	10,019,055	9,247,360	3,961,087	538,382,191
Piedmont	6,990,437	12,402,526	19,923,804	24,156,968	58,129,305	28,921,123	25,541,938	9,496,620	3,265,093	4,280,521	0	0	193,108,335
Total	257,899,170	406,112,531	569,571,583	842,568,383	1,004,323,800	815,035,222	468,551,863	220,685,308	67,861,651	43,412,576	22,219,534	3,961,087	4,722,202,708

Disturbances and Threats

Each field-visited plot, FIA survey crews note any recent disturbances, natural and anthropogenic (viewed as treatments), that have occurred since the sample location was last visited, or in the past 5 years. An assessment of the disturbances that occur in longleaf pine communities and the extent of those events create a better understanding of how longleaf pine forests are being utilized and the exogenous pressures common to these forests.

Disturbances and treatments are expressed as the average annual area or volume impacted. Current estimates indicate that only 5 percent of the longleaf pine dominated forests in the Southern United States is disturbed annually (table 15). The Piedmont exhibited the lowest estimate of area disturbed annually (3 percent) while the West Coastal Plain experienced the highest rate of disturbance (6-percent disturbed annually on average). Of the 200,000 acres where a disturbance was recorded, fire was the most common and occurred on almost 166,000 acres. Fire has the most influence on the longleaf pine ecosystem, and it is often used as a management tool.

Silvicultural activities such as planting, thinning, or fertilization observed on and/or around the plot are noted as treatments by field crews. Ninety-five percent of longleaf pine dominated forests showed no signs of any treatment (table 16) during the most recent field visit. Some type of treatment is estimated to have occurred for about 225,000 acres. Cutting was the leading treatment recorded on longleaf pine dominated acres, and it occurred on an average of 91,000 acres annually, or 40 percent of the total area where any treatment was recorded.

Longleaf pine harvests (average annual cubic feet) on timberland were greatest in and around the areas in which the greatest area of longleaf pine forests were located (fig. 24). Average annual harvests on private timberland (fig. 25) mimicked the pattern found on all timberland (fig. 23). Limited harvests occurred in longleaf pine forests on publicly owned and managed timberland (fig. 26).

Invasive plants were detected on 148 longleaf pine plots in 6 Southern States, or 21 percent of all longleaf pine plots measured (fig. 27). Louisiana and Alabama had the highest proportion of invaded plots with 35 and 32 percent, respectively, while eastern Texas and Florida had the lowest percentage of invaded plots (0 and 6 percent, respectively, though the small sample size in eastern Texas should be taken into consideration when evaluating the proportions, (table 17).

Twenty-one invasive species from a predetermined list of 33 (53 in Florida) were recorded on longleaf pine plots. Japanese honeysuckle (*Lonicera japonica*) was the most frequently detected nonnative species on longleaf pine plots in all States (table 18). The common invasive vine was found on 11 percent of all longleaf pine plots surveyed, and 52 percent of all longleaf pine plots containing an invasive species.

Table 14—All-live volume of longleaf pine species on forest land by region and ownership class, 2010

Region	Ownership class							Total
	National Forest System	Fish and Wildlife Service	Department of Defense	Other Federal	State	County and municipal	Private	
	cubic feet							
Coastal plain (east)	778,570,874	85,267,714	412,411,833	69,063,200	358,660,183	33,795,382	2,252,942,995	3,990,712,181
Coastal plain (west)	277,583,753	0	30,470,435	169,478	0	12,501,250	217,657,275	538,382,192
Piedmont	55,502,672	0	1,119,737	2,613,303	22,261,559	0	111,611,063	193,108,335
Total	1,111,657,300	85,267,714	444,002,005	71,845,982	380,921,742	46,296,633	2,582,211,333	4,722,202,708

Numbers in rows and columns may not sum to toals due to rounding.

0.0 = no sample for the cell or a value of >0.0 but <0.05.

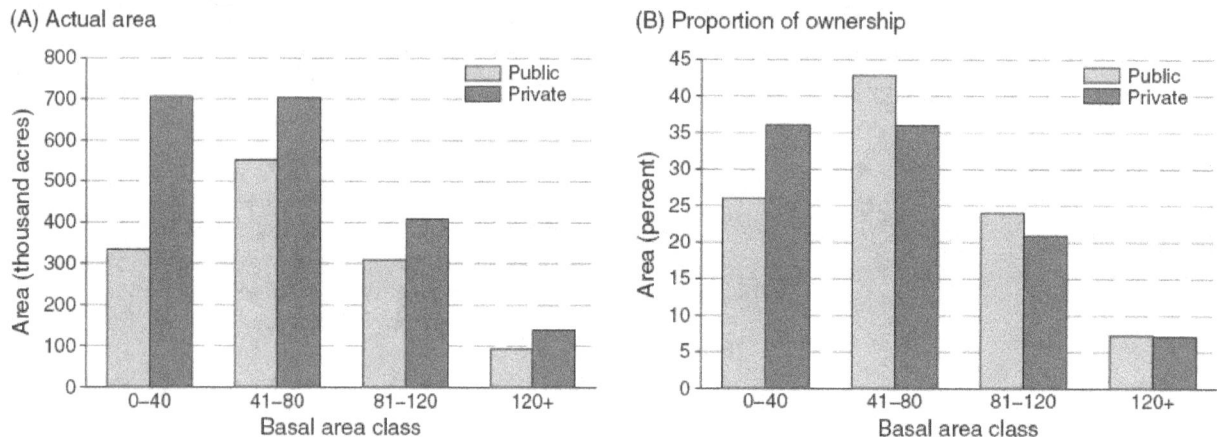

Figure 23—Forest land area by basal area class and ownership category (A) Actual area and (B) Proportion of ownership, 2010.

On average, Japanese honeysuckle foliage had an aerial coverage of 15 percent on the longleaf pine subplots on which it was found. Chinese and European privets (*Ligustrum sinense* Lour. and *L. vulgare* L.) were the second most commonly detected invasive plants, with 39 plot detections (table 18).

Tallowtree (*Triadica sebifera*) and mimosa (*Albizia julibrissin*) were the most common invasive trees found on longleaf pine plots throughout the South, with 15 and 13 detections, respectively. Tallowtree was found primarily in Louisiana and Alabama (17 and 5 percent of longleaf pine plots, respectively), and on one longleaf pine plot in Mississippi. Mimosa was found primarily in Georgia and Alabama (4 and 3 percent of longleaf pine plots, respectively).

Chinese/European privet was the only shrub detected on more than two longleaf pine plots in any State (table 18). The species was noted on 15 percent of longleaf pine plots in Georgia, 8 percent of longleaf pine plots in Alabama, 7 percent in Louisiana and North Carolina, 6 percent of longleaf pine plots in Mississippi, and 1 percent of plots in Florida and South Carolina. The only State where Chinese/European privet was not detected on at least one longleaf pine plot was Texas.

Japanese honeysuckle was the only invasive vine noted on more than two longleaf pine plots in any State (table 18). The vine was found on 20 percent of longleaf pine plots in Alabama, 15 percent in Georgia, North Carolina, and South Carolina, 12 percent in Mississippi, 7 percent in Louisiana, and 2 percent in Florida.

Table 15—Area of forest land by longleaf pine forest type, region, and disturbance class, 2010

Forest type and region	Total	Disturbance class							
		Insects	Disease	Weather	Fire	Domestic animals	Wild animals	Human	Other natural
		thousand acres							
Longleaf									
Coastal plain (east)	131.9	0.5	1.0	13.2	110.9	0.5	0.0	5.9	0.0
Coastal plain (west)	16.3	0.0	0.0	0.0	15.7	0.0	0.0	0.6	0.0
Piedmont	3.3	0.0	0.0	0.0	3.3	0.0	0.0	0.0	0.0
Total	151.5	0.5	1.0	13.2	129.9	0.5	0.0	6.4	0.0
Longleaf-oak									
Coastal plain (east)	39.0	0.0	1.4	0.8	32.3	0.4	0.0	3.3	0.9
Coastal plain (west)	1.7	0.0	0.0	0.0	1.7	0.0	0.0	0.0	0.0
Piedmont	3.0	0.0	0.0	0.0	1.7	0.0	0.0	1.4	0.0
Total	43.7	0.0	1.4	0.8	35.6	0.4	0.0	4.6	0.9
Combined longleaf									
Coastal plain (east)	170.9	0.5	2.3	14.0	143.2	0.9	0.0	9.1	0.9
Coastal plain (west)	18.0	0.0	0.0	0.0	17.4	0.0	0.0	0.6	0.0
Piedmont	6.3	0.0	0.0	0.0	5.0	0.0	0.0	1.4	0.0
Total	195.2	0.5	2.3	14.0	165.6	0.9	0.0	11.1	0.9

Numbers in rows and columns may not sum to toals due to rounding.
0.0 = no sample for the cell or a value of >0.0 but <0.05.

Table 16—Area of forest land by longleaf pine forest type, region, and treatment class, 2010

Forest type and region	Total	Treatment class									
		Final harvest	Partial harvest	Seedtree/ shelter-wood harvest	Com-mercial thinning	Timber stand improve-ment	Salvage cutting	Site prepa-ration	Artificial regen-eration	Natural regen-eration	Other silvi-cultural
		thousand acres									
Longleaf											
Coastal plain (east)	148.9	16.3	9.3	0.9	23.5	9.0	0.0	20.7	37.4	1.8	30.0
Coastal plain (west)	15.0	3.2	0.8	0.0	2.2	0.0	0.0	2.0	3.5	0.0	3.3
Piedmont	8.6	0.0	0.0	0.0	4.6	0.0	0.0	1.6	2.4	0.0	0.0
Total	172.5	19.4	10.0	0.9	30.3	9.0	0.0	24.2	43.4	1.8	33.3
Longleaf-oak											
Coastal plain (east)	43.6	7.5	5.1	1.0	4.7	0.0	0.0	9.2	10.6	1.6	3.9
Coastal plain (west)	1.4	0.4	0.0	0.0	0.0	0.5	0.0	0.0	0.0	0.4	0.0
Piedmont	7.3	2.0	0.0	0.0	0.0	0.0	0.0	2.2	2.2	1.0	0.0
Total	52.3	9.9	5.1	1.0	4.7	0.5	0.0	11.4	12.7	3.0	3.9
Combined longleaf											
Coastal plain (east)	192.5	23.8	14.4	1.9	28.3	9.0	0.0	29.9	48.0	3.4	33.9
Coastal plain (west)	16.4	3.6	0.8	0.0	2.2	0.5	0.0	2.0	3.5	0.4	3.3
Piedmont	15.9	2.0	0.0	0.0	4.6	0.0	0.0	3.7	4.6	1.0	0.0
Total	224.7	29.4	15.1	1.9	35.1	9.4	0.0	35.6	56.1	4.8	37.2

Numbers in rows and columns may not sum to toals due to rounding.
0.0 = no sample for the cell or a value of >0.0 but <0.05.

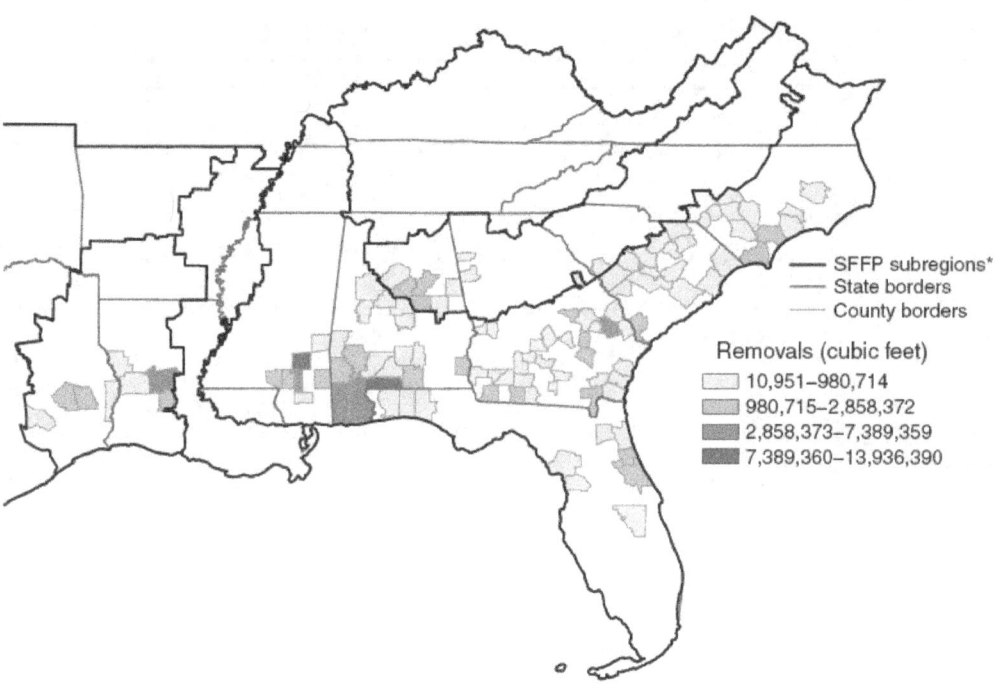

* Southern Forests Futures Project delineations (Wear and others 2009).

Figure 24—Average annual harvest removals of longleaf pine on all timberland, 2010.

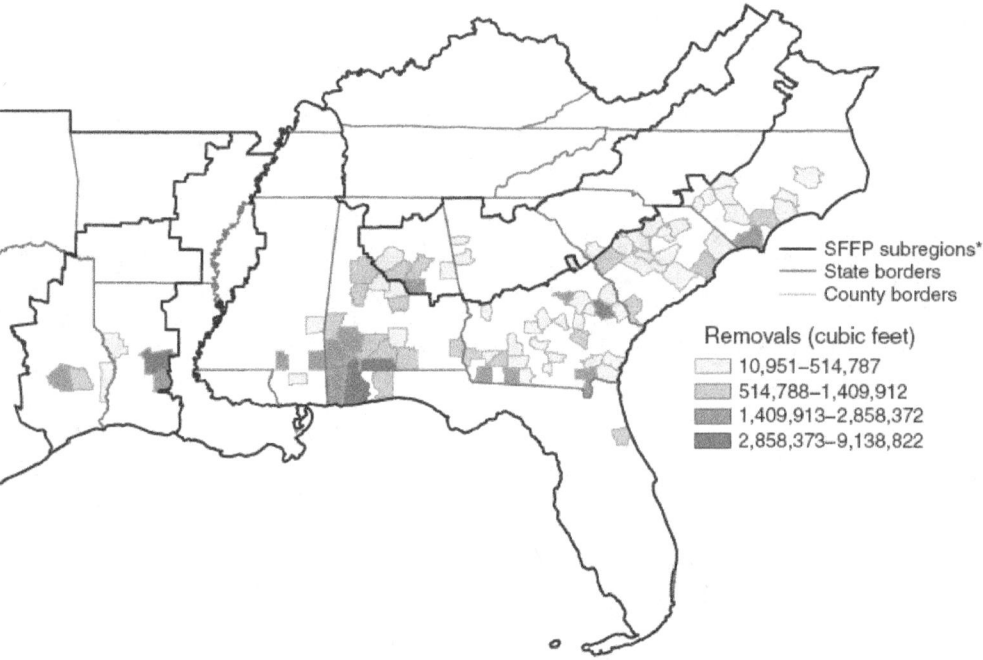

* Southern Forests Futures Project delineations (Wear and others 2009).

Figure 25—Average annual harvest removals of longleaf pine on private timberland, 2010.

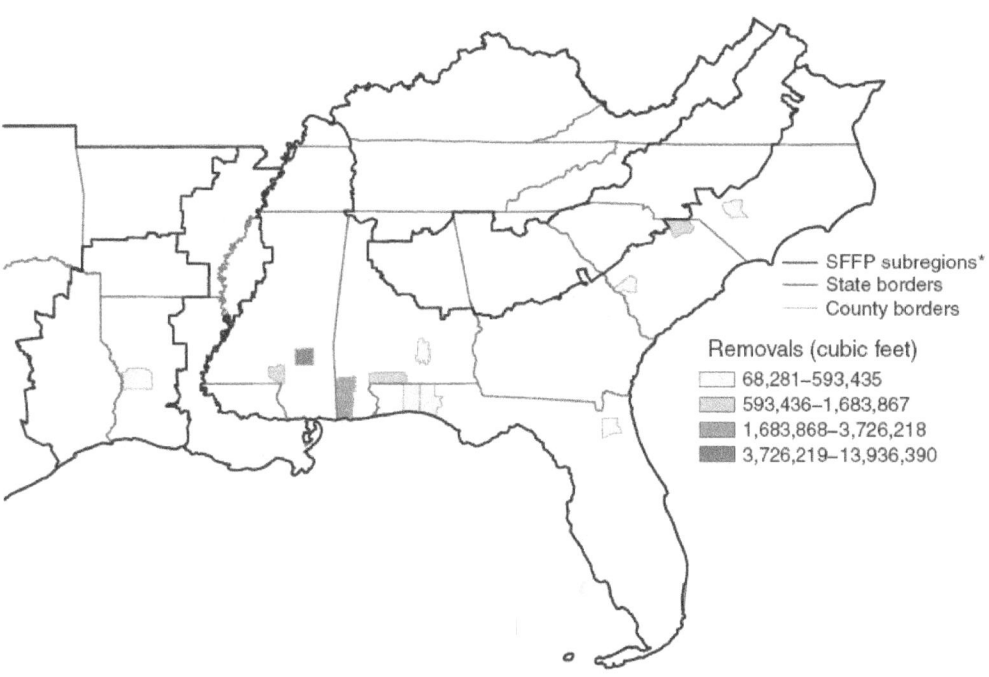

SFFP subregions*
State borders
County borders

Removals (cubic feet)
68,281–593,435
593,436–1,683,867
1,683,868–3,726,218
3,726,219–13,936,390

* Southern Forests Futures Project delineations (Wear and others 2009).

Figure 26—Average annual harvest removals of longleaf pine on public timberland, 2010.

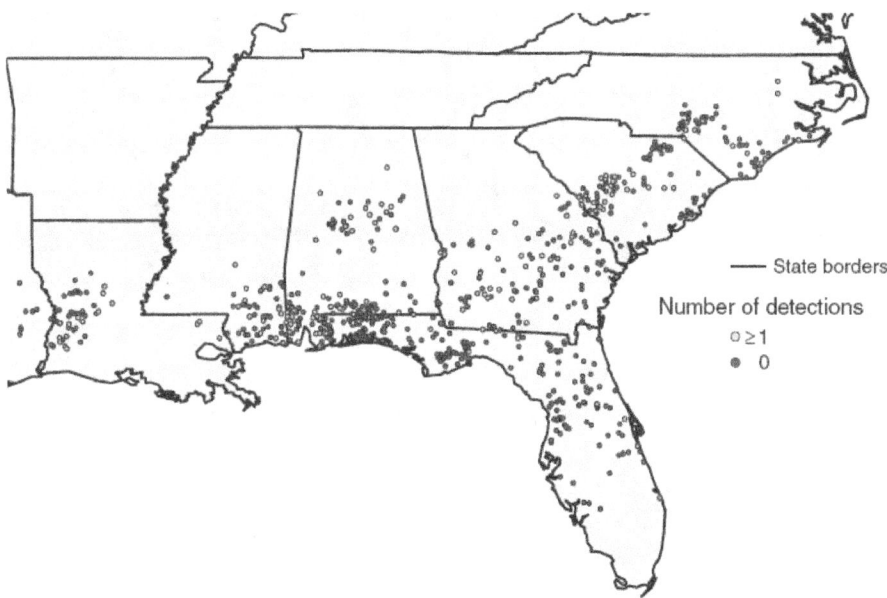

State borders

Number of detections
≥1
0

Figure 27—Presence or absence of invasive plant species on longleaf pine plots, 2010.

Table 17—Number and percent of longleaf pine plots with one or more invasive plant species detection by State, 2010

State	Longleaf pine plots with one or more invasive species	Longleaf pine plots	Longleaf pine plots with one or more invasives
	- - - - - - - number - - - - - - -		- - percent - -
Alabama	43	133	32
Florida	12	194	6
Georgia	29	109	27
Louisiana	16	46	35
Mississippi	13	50	26
North Carolina	13	60	22
South Carolina	21	89	24
East Texas	0	8	0
Total	148	689	21

Numbers in columns may not sum to toals due to rounding.

Cogongrass (*Imperata cylindrical*) was the only invasive grass noted on more than one longleaf pine plot in any State, and it was only found on more than one plot in Alabama. There, it was noted on 8 percent of longleaf pine plots. Japanese climbing fern (*Lygodium japonicum*) was the only fern noted on any longleaf pine plot. It was noted on 20 percent of longleaf pine plots in Louisiana, 14 percent in Mississippi, 7 percent in Alabama, and 4 and 2 percent in Georgia and Florida, respectively.

The only forb found on >3 percent of longleaf pine plots in any given State was Chinese lespedeza (*Lespedeza cuneata*), which was detected on 12 percent of longleaf pine plots in North Carolina, and 8 percent of longleaf plots in South Carolina. It was found on ≤2 percent of longleaf pine plots in the other States where it was observed (table 18).

Bolting longleaf pine seedlings clustered in a forest canopy gap in South Carolina. (photo by Bill Boyer, U.S. Forest Service)

Table 18—Invasive species detected on longleaf pine plots by State with frequency of plot detections and mean percent subplot cover, 2010

Species	State																	
	Alabama		Florida		Georgia		Louisiana		Mississippi		North Carolina		South Carolina		Total	
	n	mean percent	n	mean percent	n	mean percent	n	mean percent	n	mean percent	n	mean percent	n	mean percent	n	mean percent
Trees																
Tree-of-heaven	1	<1	—		—		—		—		—		—		1	<1
Silktree, mimosa	4	29	3	5	4	9	—		1	5	—		1	<1	13	14
Chinaberry	1	<1	—		4	17	—		—		—		—		5	13
Tallowtree, popcorntree	6	4	—		—		8	4	1	<1	—		—		15	4
Brazilian pepper[a]	—		1	<1	—		—		—		—		—		1	<1
Shrubs																
Chinese/European privet	10	21	2	15	16	7	3	7	3	4	4	15	1	3	39	12
Japanese/glossy privet	2	18	—		—		1	<1	1	30	—		—		4	17
Bush honeysuckles	—		—		—		1	<1	—		—		—		1	<1
Sacred bamboo, nandina	—		—		—		2	2	—		—		—		2	<1
Nonnative roses	—		—		1	5	—		—		1	5	—		2	5
Vines																
Nonnative climbing yams/ air yam/Chinese yam	1	<1	—		—		—		—		—		—		1	<1
English ivy	—		—		1	<1	—		—		—		2	63	3	42
Japanese honeysuckle	26	19	4	20	16	9	3	2	6	1	9	10	13	24	77	15
Chinese/Japanese wisteria	—		1	5	—		—		—		—		—		1	5
Grasses																
Cogongrass	10	22	1	<1	—		—		1	5	—		—		12	19
Nepalese browntop	—		—		1	<1	—		1	30	—		—		2	15
Ferns																
Japanese climbing fern	9	8	4	9	4	<1	9	3	7	8	—		—		33	6
Forbs																
Garlic mustard	—		—		—		—		—		1	<1	—		1	<1
Shrubby lespedeza	3	2	—		2	1	—		1	<1	—		2	18	8	6
Chinese lespedeza	1	5	1	5	2	<1	—		1	5	7	11	7	10	19	9
Tropical soda apple	—		—		3	4	—		—		—		1	5	4	4

[a] Collected only in Florida.

n = frequency of plot detections.

Future Research Needs

The vast longleaf pine forests of the South were under intense pressure from logging and were well on their way to extirpation just as the U.S. Forest Service began establishing research centers throughout the country. Seven centers built between 1934 and 1947 were located within the native range of longleaf pine, and research on the species was conducted at four of them. Work at the Alexandria, Louisiana center focused on artificial reforestation techniques, growth and yield of planted pines, and range research, while at Gulfport, Mississippi, scientists studied fire behavior and initiated seed source studies. Research at Brewton, Alabama examined natural regeneration of longleaf pine, the silvicultural techniques needed to manage natural stands, and the management problems of small landowners. Studies on the use of longleaf pine for naval stores began in Stark, Florida and continued into the 1970s at Lake City, Florida when the effort at Stark, Florida ended.[1] Work on longleaf pine tree improvement and genetics was also performed at Lake City, Florida.

While most of the information produced from these basic studies is still applicable to the management of longleaf pine forests, the needs of today's landowners are much broader, and research must focus on a wider range of topics (Brockway and others 2005). These were summarized in a general manner in the rangewide conservation plan for longleaf pine (Darden and others 2009). The plan was a collaborative effort in which >20 organizations and agencies participated. Its intent was to coordinate longleaf pine conservation efforts and to spark partnership formation among participants. Toward that end, the U.S. Departments of Agriculture, Defense, and the Interior signed a Memorandum of Understanding in 2010 that would promote the rangewide plan's objective of establishing an additional 5 million acres of longleaf pine forests in the next 15 years. With >80 percent of the forested land in the longleaf pine range in private hands, this is an ambitious goal. What follows is a research synopsis developed in late 2010 by a Forest Service working group in response to the rangewide plan.

Classification and Assessment

Establishing a monitoring strategy and a system to categorize longleaf pine restoration accomplishments are necessary first steps for such efforts. Standards that classify longleaf pine stands in varying stages of development and that accurately depict conditions in the field will facilitate tracking of restoration activities. This would be followed by an inventory of longleaf pine stands throughout the range of the species, including a catalog of existing longleaf pine demonstration areas on both public and private land. Development of an online tool to distribute information about the demonstration sites that would also allow Web visitors to take virtual tours of the areas could promote restoration efforts. If historical photographs or records of the areas exist that show them prior to application of silvicultural prescriptions, visitors would be able to visualize the effects of treatments and their impact if applied under varying management intensities. The monitoring system could also include forest health metrics. This would enable scientists to monitor existing or potential threats to the longleaf pine ecosystems, including invasive species, fragmentation, and land conversion. This could also be used as a predictive tool to identify future threats to these ecosystems.

Social Science and Marketing

Societal perceptions of the Nation's forests change as values and demographics shift. A strong case for restoration and conservation of longleaf pine ecosystems includes an explanation of what makes longleaf pine forests different from other forested areas and why it is in the best interests of society to maintain these ecosystems. The more information that can be gathered on public decision-making practices as they pertain to forestry issues, the better a case can be made for marketing longleaf pine restoration as worthy of taxpayer investment. A list of the services and products longleaf pine ecosystems offer that focuses exclusively on timber industry may not garner the necessary public support for restoration efforts. Additional market data and development of new markets for nontimber products [pine straw, seed collection (pines, herbaceous species), agroforestry opportunities, biomass/biofuels (market analyses), carbon credits, wildlife viewing, water, hunting] would demonstrate the value of stacked services and products from managed longleaf pine forests and make a strong case for restoration.

Demographic information on the longleaf pine region most often focuses on landowners, but it is misleading to consider the region from this aspect alone. The target audience for education may be residents of the area who do not own forested tracts but who may be negatively affected by active management activities (i.e., fire and the resulting smoke management issues). If stand management and the results thereof are perceived as threats, restoration activities may be

---

[1] Personal communication. 2011. J.P. Barnett, Emeritus Scientist, Southern Research Station, U.S. Forest Service, 2500 Shreveport Highway, Pineville, LA 71360.

A longleaf pine forest in Louisiana treated with the shelterwood method (residual basal area 25–30 square feet per acre). (photo by Bill Boyer, U.S. Forest Service)

severely curtailed. The more that is known about residents of the area, the better researchers can focus on developing management tools that will be accepted by them. In addition, no matter how sophisticated the management tool, if it is not accessible and easy to use it may be of minimal value. Demographic information could aid in development of tools that have utility for the majority of the region's residents.

Models

Landowners and managers require tools that accurately predict longleaf pine stand behavior and production. In order to manage for the future, proponents of longleaf pine restoration need various models to demonstrate the species' competitive long-term productivity and that advocate its active management. Growth and mortality models for both artificially and naturally regenerated longleaf pine are vital to restoration efforts, as is the updating of these models with continuous remeasurement data from established studies to at least a rotation age of 120 years (as specified for national forests).

Assumptions have been made that longleaf pine will survive changing climatic conditions, either maintaining or expanding its current range. Testing the validity of these assumptions will enable researchers to accurately

predict longleaf pine's adaptability to future conditions. Additionally, models of how carbon is stored above- and below-ground in longleaf pine ecosystems will facilitate assessment of the carbon sequestration potential of longleaf pine forests, including carbon budgets and the financial dimensions of longleaf pine productivity relative to economic analyses of product valuation. A fully developed model will couple biological, ecological, and economic aspects of longleaf pine restoration and management.

Risk assessment models with actuarial analysis of risk avoidance could be used to analyze forest threats, such as wildfire, insects, diseases, and wind events as well as examine alternative silvicultural treatments for mitigating or avoiding these problems. If fire is a necessary component of the system, the development of accessible and user-friendly models dealing with the complexities of smoke management will be needed. Such models may also demonstrate tradeoffs of alternative management strategies in the WUI.

Management

Information on seed production, seed collection, and nursery production is essential if the goal of planting millions of acres in longleaf pine is to be met. To this end, longleaf pine genetic variation needs to be examined. Researchers have not determined if there is a genetic component to cone production in longleaf pine, nor is it known if tree provenance relates to cone and seed production. Currently, longleaf pine seed transfer is based on provenance and progeny tests conducted decades ago. A new comprehensive provenance and progeny project has been initiated, and these efforts need to be supported. Along these lines, the species should be studied for genetic benchmarks that relate to short- and long-term field performance.

Best nursery guidelines and protocols for increased production of high quality longleaf pine seedlings and for maximizing the early field performance of planted seedlings on a variety of soils and sites should be developed and disseminated. Test sites evaluating stock quality and early field performance of container-grown and bareroot longleaf pine seedlings from across the South should be established, as should studies of different longleaf pine planting stock in areas that are hurricane prone versus safer zones. Knowledge of the physiological and morphological responses of young longleaf pine to climate change may be essential to restoration efforts.

The debate on the necessity of fire in management of longleaf pine stands continues and could be resolved by formation of a decision support system on whether or not to burn, and under what conditions. A rangewide system could contain updated recommendations on season of burn to minimize negative effects on longleaf pine growth and assessments of fuel bed and fire intensity interactions on tree growth and survival. Such a tool would enable managers to tailor the season of prescribed fire to their site conditions for sustained longleaf pine carbon sequestration. Methods for restoring fire to long-unburned longleaf pine stands on varying sites should also be addressed.

The list of basic practical research needs is extensive and includes issues that range from controlling native and exotic weeds in longleaf pine stands during early establishment and new studies for uneven-aged/alternative management techniques for longleaf pine stands to red-cockaded woodpecker and herpetology management guidelines. Included in this mix of topics are:

• Assessment of the current state of the longleaf pine resource and of longleaf pine forests of the United States and trends in pine productivity in the Southeast since 1970.

• Guidelines for longleaf pine stand establishment on wet sites, silvopasture holdings, and sites with soil resource limitations.

• Silvicultural guidance for forest managers to achieve sustainable even- and uneven-aged longleaf pine stands and to determine if the benefits of high quality systems versus altered conditions offset management's costs.

• Recommendations for gradual conversion of loblolly pine stands to longleaf pine stands.

• Evaluation of mature longleaf pine wood quality in response to stand density management.

• Identification of the overlap between strategic longleaf pine restoration areas and strategic bioenergy areas.

• Evaluation of longleaf pine's physiological response to seasonal prescribed burning and to climate change factors.

Understory

The richly diverse fire-dependent understory communities in longleaf pine ecosystems carry fire through the system and provide essential habitat for fauna. Because fire use has been infrequent and other management practices were not favorable to understory vegetation, it is suspected that ground layer communities are in poor condition throughout much of the longleaf pine range, yet the practical tools for their restoration are undeveloped. Their formation is key for meeting agency goals and objectives.

Seed transfer zones for longleaf pine herbaceous ground layer associates have been tentatively mapped (Walker and Hernández 2010), but their precise delineation awaits results from common garden studies and direct genetic assessments. Guidelines for managing ground layer vegetation in natural systems for reliable grass seed production await development as do seed germination and storage protocols, seed collection guidelines for public lands, provisional seed handling/transfer guidelines, and plans for seed marketing.

The influence of silvicultural treatments on understory plants could be exemplified by a network of sites demonstrating restoration protocols for existing longleaf pine plantations. This would enable researchers to display various methods for establishing ground layer vegetation in stands of varying age with different establishment and management history, management objectives, and environmental conditions. Evaluations of herbicide effects on desirable nontarget herbaceous species of the longleaf pine ground layer community could be included in these demonstration plots.

Conclusions

Longleaf pine was once one of the most ecologically important tree species, if not the most ecologically important tree species, in the Southern United States. That, of course, is not the case today. Longleaf pine, and its associated longleaf pine forest ecosystems, are now scarce across the southern forest landscape. Today, only 4.3 million acres of longleaf pine dominated forests remain in a region where these forests once covered nearly 92 million acres. While longleaf pine dominated forests have received considerable attention and land managers and conservation professionals are working to maintain and improve these important systems, longleaf pine forests currently only occupy a minor portion of the southern landscape. That said, there are positive signs in this report that point toward potential improvements. For example, the number of longleaf pine saplings has been increasing, the longleaf pine/oak acreage represents a considerable opportunity for restoration to longleaf pine forests, and in some areas of the longleaf pine range young stands are developing to aid replacement of those lost. Significant challenges to expanding the coverage of longleaf pine dominated forests do exist. However, with targeted research and conservation efforts, longleaf pine forests can thrive once again across the South.

Literature Cited

Anderson, M.K. 1996. Tending the wilderness. Restoration and Management Notes. 14: 154–166.

Bartram, W. 1791. Travel through North and South Carolina, Georgia and East and West Florida. New York: Dover Publishers. 414 p.

Bechtold, W.A.; Patterson, P.L., eds. 2005. The enhanced forest inventory and analysis program—national sampling design and estimation procedures. Gen. Tech. Rep. SRS–80. Asheville, NC: U.S. Department of Agriculture Forest Service, Southern Research Station. 85 p.

Beers, T.W.; Miller, C.I. 1964. Point sampling: research results, theory and applications. Res. Bull. 786. Lafayette, IN: Purdue University Agricultural Experiment Station. 55 p.

Boyer, W.D. 1990. *Pinus palustris* Mill. longleaf pine. In: Burns, R.M.; Honkala, B.H., tech. coord. Silvics of North America. Vol. 1, Conifers. Washington, DC: U.S. Department of Agriculture Forest Service: 405–412.

Brockway, D.G.; Lewis, C.E. 1997. Long-term effects of dormant-season prescribed fire on plant community diversity, structure and productivity in a longleaf pine wiregrass ecosystem. Forest Ecology and Management. 96(1, 2): 167–183.

Brockway, D.G.; Outcalt, K.W. 2000. Restoring longleaf pine wiregrass ecosystems: hexazinone application enhances effects of prescribed fire. Forest Ecology and Management. 137(1–3): 121–138.

A longleaf pine stand on a flatwoods site in Florida treated by single-tree selection using the Pro-B Method. (photo by Dale Brockway, U.S. Forest Service)

Brockway, D.G.; Outcalt, K.W.; Estes, B.L.; Rummer, R.B. 2009. Vegetation response to midstorey mulching and prescribed burning for wildfire hazard reduction and longleaf pine (*Pinus palustris* Mill.) ecosystem restoration. Forestry. 82(3): 299–314.

Brockway, D.G.; Outcalt, K.W.; Tomczak, D.J.; Johnson, E.E. 2005. Restoration of longleaf pine ecosystems. Gen. Tech. Rep. SRS–83. Asheville, NC: U.S. Department of Agriculture Forest Service, Southern Research Station. 34 p.

Carr, S.C.; Robertson, K.M.; Peet, R.K. 2010. A vegetation classification of fire-dependent pinelands of Florida. Castanea. 75(2): 153–189.

Carroll, W.D.; Kapeluck, P.R.; Harper, R.A.; Van Lear, D.H. 2002. Historical overview of the southern forest landscape and associated resources. In: Wear, D.N.; Greis, J.G., eds. The southern forest resource assessment. Gen. Tech. Rep. SRS–53. Asheville, NC: U.S. Department of Agriculture Forest Service, Southern Research Station: 583–605.

Croker, T.C. 1987. Longleaf pine: a history of man and a forest. Forestry Rep. R8–FR7. Atlanta: U.S. Department of Agriculture Forest Service, Southern Region. 37 p.

Darden, T.; Case, D.; Hayes, L. [and others]. 2009. Range-wide conservation plan for longleaf pine. Regional working group for longleaf pine. America's longleaf, a restoration initiative for the southern longleaf pine forest. 42 p. http://www.flyways.us/sites/default/files/uploads/conservation_plan.pdf. [Date accessed unknown].

Delcourt, P.A. 1980. Goshen Springs: late quaternary vegetation record for southern Alabama. Ecology. 61(2): 372–386.

Delcourt, P.A.; Delcourt, H.R. 1987. Long-term forest dynamics of the temperate zone. New York: Springer-Verlag. 439 p.

Diop, A.; Palola, E.; Staudt, A.; Stein, B. 2009. Standing tall: how restoring longleaf pine can help prepare the Southeast for global warming. Reston, VA: National Wildlife Federation. 21 p.

Drew M.B.; Kirkman, L.K.; Gholson, A.K. 1998. The vascular flora of Ichauway, Baker County, Georgia: a remnant longleaf pine/wiregrass ecosystem. Castanea. 63: 1–24.

Estill, J.C.; Cruzan, M. 2001. Phytogeography of rare plant species endemic to the Southeastern United States. Castanea. 66(1–2): 3–23.

Franklin, R.M. 1997. Stewardship of longleaf pine forests: a guide for landowners. Longleaf Alliance Report No. 2. Andalusia, AL: Solon Dixon Forestry Education Center. 44 p.

Franzreb, K.E.; Oswalt, S.N.; Buehler, D.A. 2011. Population trends for eastern scrub-shrub birds related to availability of small-diameter upland hardwood forests. In: Greenberg, C.; Collins, B.; Thompson, F., eds. Ecology and management of early successional habitats in the central hardwood region, USA series: managing forest ecosystems, Vol. 21. 1st ed. New York: Springer: 143–166.

Frayer, W.E.; Furnival, G.M. 2000. History of forest survey sampling designs in the United States. In: Hansen, M.; Burk, T., eds. Integrated tools for natural resources inventories in the 21st century. Gen. Tech. Rep. NC–212. St. Paul, MN: U.S. Dept. of Agriculture Forest Service, North Central Forest Experiment Station: 42–49.

Frost, C.C. 1993. Four centuries of changing landscape patterns in the longleaf pine ecosystem. In: Hermann, S.M., ed. Proceedings of the 18th Tall Timbers fire ecology conference: the longleaf pine ecosystem: ecology, restoration and management. Tallahassee, FL: Tall Timbers Research Station: 17–43.

Frost, C. 2006. History and future of the longleaf pine ecosystem. In: Jose, S.; Jokela, E.J.; Miller, D.L., eds. The longleaf ecosystem: ecology, silviculture and restoration. New York: Springer Science: 9–48.

Greenberg, C.H.; Simons, R.W. 1999. Age, composition and stand structure of old-growth oak sites in the Florida high pine landscape: implications for ecosystem management and restoration. Natural Areas Journal. 19(1): 30–40.

Grosenbaugh, L.R. 1952. Plotless timber estimates—new, fast, easy. Journal of Forestry. 50: 32–37.

Harcombe, P.A.; Glitzenstein, J.S.; Knox, R.G. [and others]. 1993. Vegetation of the longleaf pine region of the west gulf coast plain. In: Hermann, S M., ed. Proceedings of the 18th Tall Timbers fire ecology conference: the longleaf pine ecosystem: ecology, restoration and management. Tallahassee, FL: Tall Timbers Research Station: 83–104.

Harper, W.M. 1913. A defense of forest fires. Literary Digest. 47: 208.

Hart, J.F. 1979. The role of the plantation in southern agriculture. In: Proceedings of the 16th Tall Timbers fire ecology conference. Tallahassee, FL: Tall Timbers Research Station: 1–19.

Hilliard, T. 1998. Longleaf-wiregrass restoration at Fort Stewart, Georgia: the military's role in restoration. In: Kush, J.S., comp. ed. Ecological restoration and regional conservation strategies. Longleaf Alliance Rep. No. 3. Andalusia, AL: Solon Dixon Forestry Education Center. 32 p.

Hindle, B. 1975. America's wooden age: aspects of its early technology. Tarrytown, NY: Sleepy Hollow Restorations. 218 p.

Kelly, J.F.; Bechtold, W.A. 1990. The longleaf pine resource. In: Farrar, R.M., ed. Management of longleaf pine. Gen. Tech. Rep. SO–75. New Orleans: U.S. Department of Agriculture Forest Service, Southern Forest Experiment Station: 11–22.

Komarek, E.V. 1968. Lightning and lightning fires as ecological forces. In: Proceedings, 8th Tall Timbers ecology conference. Tallahassee, FL: Tall Timbers Research Station: 169–197.

Landers, J.L.; Boyer, W.D. 1999. An old-growth definition for upland longleaf and south Florida slash pine forests, woodlands and savannas. Gen. Tech. Rep. SRS–29. Asheville, NC: U.S. Department of Agriculture Forest Service, Southern Research Station. 15 p.

Landers, J.L.; Byrd, N.A.; Komarek, R. 1990. A holistic approach to managing longleaf pine communities. In: Farrar, R.M., ed. Management of longleaf pine. Gen. Tech. Rep. SO–75. New Orleans: U.S. Department of Agriculture Forest Service, Southern Forest Experiment Station: 135–167.

Landers, J.L.; Van Lear, D.H.; Boyer, W.D. 1995. The longleaf pine forests of the Southeast: requiem or renaissance? Journal of Forestry. 93(11): 39–44.

LeBlond, R.J. 2001. Endemic plants of the Cape Fear Arch region. Castanea. 66(1–2): 83–97.

Little, E.L., Jr. 1971. Atlas of United States trees. Volume 1. Conifers and important hardwoods. Misc. Publ. 1146. Washington, DC: U.S. Department of Agriculture Forest Service. 9 p. 200 maps.

McMahon, C.K.; Tomczak, D.J.; Jeffers, R.M. 1998. Longleaf pine ecosystem restoration: the role of the USDA Forest Service. In: Kush, J.S., comp. ed. Ecological restoration and regional conservation strategies. Longleaf Alliance Report No. 3. Andalusia, AL: Solon Dixon Forestry Education Center: 20–31.

Mohr, C.T. 1897. The timber pines of the southern United States. Bull. No. 13. Washington, DC: U.S. Department of Agriculture Division of Forestry. 176 p.

Noss, R.F.; LaRoe, E.T.; Scott, J.M. 1995. Endangered ecosystems of the United States: a preliminary assessment of loss and degradation. Biological Rep. 28. Washington, DC: U.S. Department of Interior, National Biological Service. 59 p.

Outcalt, K.W. 1997. Status of the longleaf pine forests of the West Gulf Coastal Plain. Texas Journal of Science. 49(3) Supplement: 5–12.

Outcalt, K.W. 1998. Needs and opportunities for longleaf pine ecosystem restoration in Florida. In: Kush, J.S., comp. ed. Ecological restoration and regional conservation strategies. Longleaf Alliance Rep. No. 3. Andalusia, AL: Solon Dixon Forestry Education Center: 38–43.

Outcalt, K.W. 2000. Occurrence of fire in longleaf pine stands in the southeastern United States. In: Moser, W.K.; Moser, C.F., eds. Proceedings of the 21st Tall Timbers fire ecology conference: fire and forest ecology: innovative silviculture and vegetation management. Tallahassee, FL: Tall Timbers Research Station: 178–182.

Outcalt, K.W.; Brockway, D.G. 2010. Structure and composition changes following restoration treatments of longleaf pine forests on the Gulf Coastal Plain of Alabama. Forest Ecology and Management. 259: 1615–1623.

Outcalt, K.W.; Sheffield, R.M. 1996. The longleaf pine forest: trends and current conditions. Resour. Bull. SRS–9. Asheville, NC: U.S. Department of Agriculture Forest Service, Southern Research Station. 23 p.

Palik, B.J.; Pederson, N. 1996. Overstory mortality and canopy disturbances in longleaf pine ecosystems. Canadian Journal of Forest Research. 26: 2035–2047.

Peet, R.K. 2006. Ecological classification of the longleaf pine woodlands. In: Jose, S.; Jokela, E.J.; Miller, D.L., eds. The longleaf pine ecosystem: ecology, silviculture, and restoration. New York: Springer: 51–94.

Peet, R.K.; Allard, D.J. 1993. Longleaf pine vegetation of the southern Atlantic and eastern Gulf Coast regions: a preliminary classification. In: Hermann, S M., ed. Proceedings of the 18th Tall Timbers fire ecology conference: the longleaf pine ecosystem: ecology, restoration and management. Tallahassee, FL: Tall Timbers Research Station: 45–81.

Peet, R.K.; Carr, S.; Gramling, J. 2006. Fire-adapted pineland vegetation of northern and central Florida: a framework for inventory, management, and restoration. Final Report. Project NG 98–016. Tallahassee, FL: Florida Fish and Wildlife Commission. [Number of pages unknown].

Provencher, L.; Litt, A.R.; Galley, K.E.M. [and others]. 2001. Restoration of fire suppressed longleaf pine sandhills at Eglin Air Force Base, Niceville, Florida. Gainesville, FL: The Nature Conservancy, Science Division. 294 p.

Pyne, S.J. 1997. Fire in America: a cultural history of wildland and rural fire. Princeton, NJ: Princeton University Press. 654 p.

Reams, G.A.; Smith, W.D.; Hansen, M.H. [and others]. 2005. The forest inventory and analysis sampling frame. Gen. Tech. Rep. SRS–80. Asheville, NC: U.S. Department of Agriculture Forest Service, Southern Research Station: 21–36.

Rebertus, A.J.; Williamson, G.B.; Platt, W.J. 1993. The impact of temporal variation in fire regime on savanna oaks and pines. In: Hermann, S.M., ed. Proceedings of the 18th Tall Timbers fire ecology conference: the longleaf pine ecosystem: ecology, restoration and management. Tallahassee, FL: Tall Timbers Research Station: 215–225.

Robbins, L.E.; Myers, R.L. 1992. Seasonal effects of prescribed burning in Florida: a review. Misc. Publ. No. 8. Tallahassee, FL: Tall Timbers Research Station. 96 p.

Schmidtling, R.C.; Hipkins, V. 1998. Genetic diversity in longleaf pine (*Pinus palustris*): influence of historical and prehistorical events. Canadian Journal of Forest Research. 28: 1135–1145.

Schultz, R.P. 1997. The ecology and culture of loblolly pine (*Pinus taeda* L.). Agric. Handb. No. 713. Washington, DC: U.S. Department of Agriculture Forest Service. 493 p.

Schwartz, M.W. 1994. Natural distribution and abundance of forest species and communities in northern Florida. Ecology. 75(3): 687–705.

Schwarz, G.F. 1907. The longleaf pine virgin forest: a silvical study. New York: John Wiley. 135 p.

Smith, W.B.; Vissage, J.S.; Darr, D.R.; Sheffield, R.M. 2001. Forest resources of the United States, 1997. Gen. Tech. Rep. NC–219. St. Paul, MN: U.S. Department of Agriculture Forest Service, North Central Research Station. 190 p.

Sorrie, B.A.; Weakley, A.S. 2006. Conservation of the endangered *Pinus palustris* ecosystem based on coastal plain centres of plant endemism. Applied Vegetation Science. 9: 59–66.

Stanturf, J.A.; Wade, D.D.; Waldrop, T.A. [and others]. 2002. Fire in southern landscapes. In: Wear, D.N.; Greis, J.G., eds. The southern forest resource assessment. Gen. Tech. Rep. SRS–53. Asheville, NC: U.S. Department of Agriculture Forest Service, Southern Research Station: 607–630.

Stout, I.J.; Marion, W.R. 1993. Pine flatwoods and xeric pine forests of the southern (lower) coastal plain. In: Martin, W.H.; Boyce, S.G.; Echternacht, A.C., eds. Biodiversity of the Southeastern United States: lowland terrestrial communities. New York: John Wiley: 373–446.

Stowe, J.P.; Varner, J.M.; McGuire, J.P. 2002. Montane longleaf pinelands. Tipularia. 17: 9–14.

Trani, M.K.; Brooks, R.T.; Schmidt, T.L. [and others]. 2001. Patterns and trends of early successional forests in the Eastern United States. Wildlife Society Bulletin. 29(2): 413–424.

U.S. Department of Agriculture Forest Service; U.S. Department of Defense; U.S. Department of Interior. 2010. Memorandum of understanding: establish a framework to provide federal leadership to achieve the goals of the America's longleaf initiative as described in the conservation plan for longleaf pine. Washington, DC. 6 p.

U.S. Department of Agriculture Forest Service. 2008. Forest inventory and analysis national core field guide: field data collection procedures for phase 2 plots. Version 4.0. Volume 1. Arlington, VA: U.S. Department of Agriculture Forest Service, Forest Inventory and Analysis Program. 203 p. www.fia.fs.fed.us/library/fieldguides-methods-proc. [Date accessed unknown].

Van Deusen, P.C.; Dell, T.R.; Thomas, C.E. 1986. Volume growth estimation from permanent horizontal points. Forest Science. 32: 415–422.

Wahlenberg, W.G. 1946. Longleaf pine: its use, ecology, regeneration, protection, growth, and management. Washington, DC: C.L. Pack Forestry Foundation; U.S. Department of Agriculture Forest Service. 429 p.

Walker, J.L. 1999. Longleaf pine forests and woodlands: old growth under fire! In: Miller, G.L., ed. The value of old growth forest ecosystems of the Eastern United States: conference proceedings. Asheville, NC: University of North Carolina: 33–40

Walker, J.; Hernández, G. 2010. Using endemicity, floristics and ecoregions to establish seed zones for longleaf understory restoration. [Poster]. In: Kush, J.S., comp. Longleaf through time: yesterday, today, tomorrow. Proceedings of the eighth longleaf alliance regional conference. Longleaf Alliance Rep. No. 16. http://www.lpsdl.auburn.edu/pdfs/8thProceedings.pdf. [Date accessed unknown].

Walker, J.; Peet, R.K. 1983. Composition and species diversity of pine-wiregrass savannas of the Green Swamp, North Carolina. Vegetatio. 55: 163–179.

Watts, W.A. 1970. The full-glacial vegetation of northwestern Georgia. Ecology. 51(1): 17–33.

Watts, W.A. 1971. Postglacial and interglacial vegetation history of southern Georgia and central Florida. Ecology. 52(4): 676–690.

Watts, W.A.; Hansen, B.C.S. 1988. Environments of Florida in the late Wisconsin and Holocene. In: Purdy, B.A., ed. Wet site archeology. Caldwell, NJ: Telford Press: 307–323.

Watts, W.A.; Hansen, B.C.S.; Grimm, E.C. 1992. Camel Lake: a 40,000-yr record of vegetational and forest history from north Florida. Ecology. 73(3): 1056–1066.

Wear, D.N.; Greis, J.G. 2002. Summary report. In: Wear, D.N.; Greis, J.G., eds. The southern forest resources assessment. Gen. Tech. Rep. SRS–53. Asheville, NC: U.S. Department of Agriculture Forest Service, Southern Research Station. 114 p.

Wear, D.N.; Greis, J.G.; Walters, N. 2009. The southern forest futures project: using public input to define the issues. Gen. Tech. Rep. SRS–115. Asheville, NC: U.S. Department of Agriculture Forest Service, Southern Research Station. 17 p.

Williams, J.L. 1837. The territory of Florida. 1962 ed. Gainesville, FL: University of Florida Press. 304 p.

Williams, M. 1989. Americans and their forests: a historical geography. New York: Cambridge University Press. 541 p.

Woudenberg, S.W.; Conkling, B.L.; O'Connell, B.M. [and others]. 2010. The forest inventory and analysis database: database description and users manual version 4.0 for phase 2. Gen. Tech. Rep. RMRS–GTR–245. Fort Collins, CO: U.S. Department of Agriculture Forest Service, Rocky Mountain Research Station. 336 p.

Appendix

Procedures

A State-by-State inventory of the Nation's forest land began in the mid-1930s. These early surveys were primarily designed and conducted to provide estimates of forest area; wood volume; and growth, removals, and mortality.

Throughout the years, national concerns over perceived and real trends in forest resource conditions, and numerous technical innovations have led to an array of improvements (Reams and others 2005). The primary purpose for conducting forest inventories has remained largely unchanged, but the methods have undergone substantial change.

Prior to 1995, the Forest Inventory and Analysis (FIA) Program of the Forest Service, U.S. Department of Agriculture, conducted surveys using a prism sampling technique for large trees, and fixed-radius subplots for smaller trees. The basic sample design was implemented nationally, but regional differences in methods and techniques existed. In 1995, the FIA program began implementing a standardized inventory design to be used nationally.

The longleaf pine resource estimates provided in this report include estimates from both periodic and annual inventories conducted between 1970 and 2010 (table 1).

The following is a general description of the current sample design and the procedures used to collect forest resource data and derive resource estimates for each State in the southern FIA region.

A brief discussion of past sample designs and procedures are included to alert users to substantive changes. Detailed information describing past inventory procedures for a particular State and survey year can be found in analytical reports published for each Southern State (www.srs.fs.usda.gov/pubs).

Sample Design

Current annual fixed-area inventory system—Beginning in 1995, the FIA program began implementing a standardized inventory design to be used nationally. The current FIA inventory is a three-phase survey conducted on an annual basis. Phase 1 (P1) procedures produce estimates of forest and nonforest area based on national land cover data.

Phase 2 (P2) procedures involve annual field visits to a portion of the fixed-radius ground sample locations (plots). At each location sampling forest land, field crews collect tree and site data used to derive estimates of forest area, wood volume, tree growth, removals, mortality, and other attributes.

A restored longleaf pine site in southern Alabama following thinning and fire. (photo by Dale Brockway, U.S. Forest Service)

All sample locations visited in a particular year are collectively referred to as a panel. Depending upon the State, a complete measurement cycle is composed of 5, 7, or 10 panels of data.

Phase 3 (P3) procedures involve sampling on a subset (1/16th) of the P2 sample locations. P3 measurements are combined with P2 measurements to assess the overall health of forested ecosystems within each State.

Previous periodic, variable-radius, and fixed-radius inventory systems—Previously, the FIA program conducted surveys one State at a time. Each statewide inventory required 1 to 3 years to complete. These "periodic" inventories were designed to provide updated forest resource estimates for all States every 7 to 10 years.

Data collection was based on a 10-point prism sampling (variable-radius) technique (Grosenbaugh 1952) for large trees, and fixed-radius (6.8 feet) subplots for smaller trees.

The basic configuration of the cluster of points varied among States and, in some cases, points were relocated to ensure that all points sampled the same forest condition. The following section offers a more detailed discussion of the changes in plot design and layout of the plot cluster.

Changes in Plot Design

Current plot design—The current annual survey design (fig. A.1) employs a cluster of four 24-foot (1/24 of an acre) fixed-radius subplots with centers spaced 120 feet apart (Bechtold and Patterson 2005). The cumulative sample area of these four subplots is one-sixth of an acre. Trees ≥5 inches diameter at breast height (d.b.h.) are measured on each subplot. Trees ≥1.0 to 4.9 inches d.b.h. and seedlings (<1.0-inch d.b.h.) are measured on a microplot (1/300 of an acre; 6.8-foot radius), offset 12 feet at 90 degrees from the subplot centers.

Unique land use and forest conditions encountered on the cluster of four subplots are delineated or "mapped" in order to isolate landscape features into homogeneous units. Forest and nonforest boundaries on the plot are mapped first.

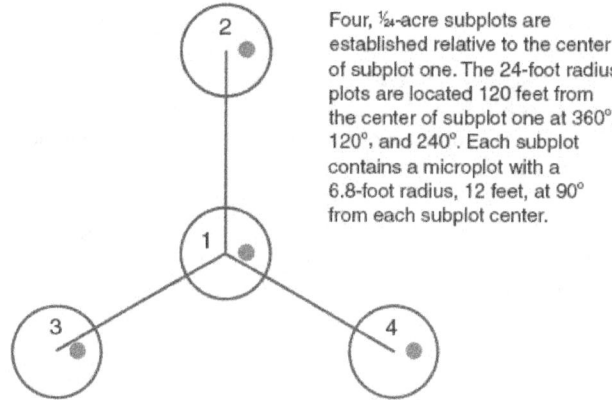

Four, ¼-acre subplots are established relative to the center of subplot one. The 24-foot radius plots are located 120 feet from the center of subplot one at 360°, 120°, and 240°. Each subplot contains a microplot with a 6.8-foot radius, 12 feet, at 90° from each subplot center.

Figure A.1—Current FIA plot design.

Then forested portions of the plot are mapped if differences in forest type, stand size, ownership, stand density, regeneration status, and reserved status can be discerned.

Previous plot design—Prior to 1995, FIA surveys used a prism sampling technique for large trees and fixed-radius subplots for smaller trees. At each forested location, survey crews installed a cluster of 10 satellite points (subplots) spaced 66 feet apart, distributed over an area about one acre.

At each subplot sampling forest, sample trees ≥5.0 inches d.b.h. were selected using a 37.5 basal-area factor (BAF) prism. Trees 1.0 to 4.9 inches d.b.h. and seedlings (<1.0-inch d.b.h.) were tallied (depending on the State being surveyed) on a 7.1-foot radius (1/275-acre) or 6.8-foot radius (1/300 acre) fixed plot that was located at the center of the three or more satellite points.

The land use sampled at plot center (subplot 1) was used to classify the entire subplot cluster. There was no mapping of forest-nonforest boundaries or delineation of forest conditions. With few exceptions, when subplot 1 sampled forest, all remaining subplots were moved or "rotated" into the same forest condition. This was done according to a predefined protocol designed to maintain the 66-foot minimum distance between sample points.

Determining Forest Resource

Statistics—Changes in sample design and plot configuration changed the derivation of basic resource statistics, e.g., forest area, stocking, growth, removals, and mortality.

The following section briefly describes the methods and processes used and explains how they have changed with the transition from the previous to the current inventory system.

Estimating Forest Area

Annual inventory system—FIA bases the three phases of the current sampling method on a hexagonal grid (hex) design (fig. A.2) with each successive phase sampled with less intensity (Bechtold and Patterson 2005). There are 16 P2 hexes for every P3 hex, and 27 P1 hexes for every P2 hex. P1 hexes represent about 222 acres, while P2

and P3 hexes represent roughly 6,000 and 96,000 acres, respectively.

Phase 1 (P1) involves assigning a single plot to the P1 hexes on digital imagery—currently FIA uses the national land cover database (NLCD). Each hex point, or "dot," is classified as either forest or nonforest, and a percentage for each class is derived for the entire State. The P1 point classifications are then checked at permanent ground sample locations that makeup the P2 sample.

Two correction factors are created by comparing the forest and nonforest classifications on the digital imagery to the classifications of the same points made at ground sample locations. These correction factors are used to adjust the percent forest derived from the original (P1) estimate. The correction factors also adjust for possible misclassifications in the NLCD, and for change on the ground that occurred since the date of the digital imagery used for land cover classification.

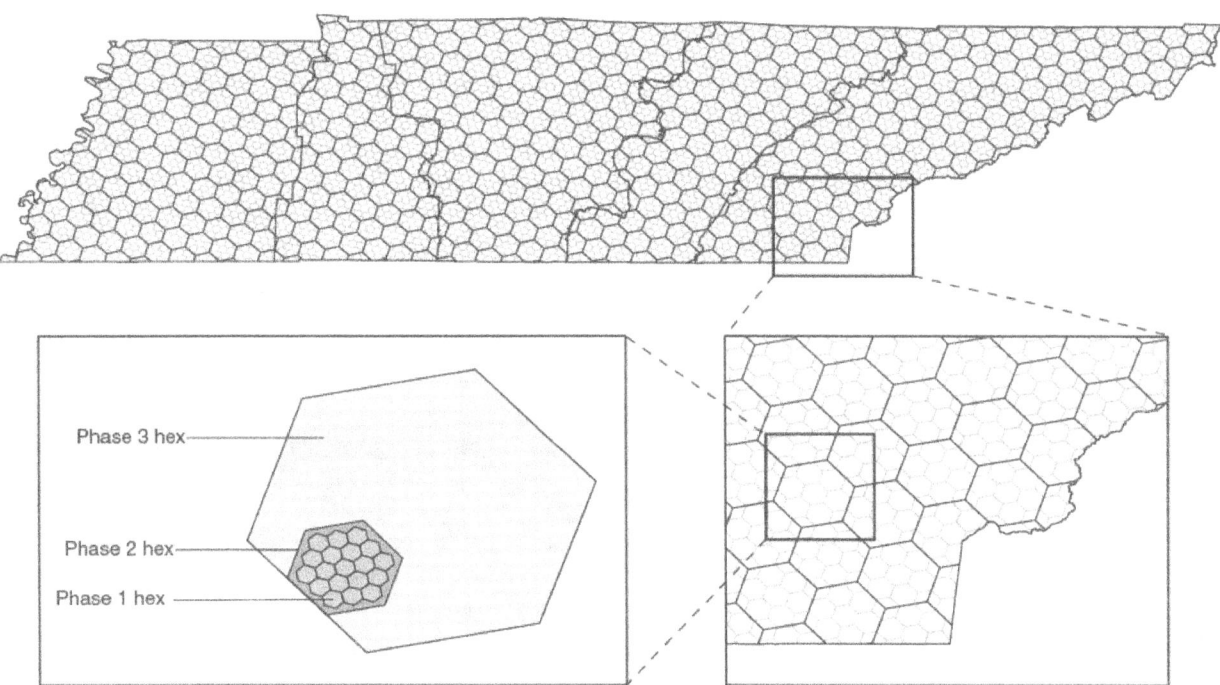

Figure A.2—Example of 3-phase hexagonal grid for FIA sampling.

Periodic inventory system—Ground sample locations were placed at the intersection of lines on a 3-mile grid lain over each State. Depending upon the survey unit sampling intensity adopted by each State, each plot represented from 2,500 acres to nearly 5,800 acres of forest land.

Area estimation was based on photointerpreting the ground use of each sample location and 25 photo sample points around each plot. The ratio of forest-to-nonforest dots provided the percent forest for each county. Field crew personnel determined the actual ground use of the plot at the time it was sampled. Percent forest for each county was calculated using the same methods and procedures used for the current survey.

Sampling intensity for some Southern States was increased by adding a 6-mile grid overlain on the 3-mile grid. The plot centers and 25 associated sample points of these plots were photointerpreted and verified by the field crews. No additional information was gathered from these locations. These plots were referred to as "supplemental" plots and their sole purpose was to strengthen the area estimation sample.

Estimating stocking, forest type, and stand-product class—FIA now uses new procedures for associating forest-type and stand-product (formerly referred to as stand-size) classes with each condition observed on a plot. The procedures, definitions, and associated algorithms are designed by FIA nationally to provide consistency among States.

The list of recognized forest types, groupings of these forest types for reporting purposes, models used to assign stocking values to individual trees, and names given to the forest types have changed over time.

Stocking (the density value assigned to a sampled live tree expressed as a percentage of the total tree density required to fully utilize the growth potential of the land) is the basis for calculating stand size and forest type. Procedures used to assign stocking to individual trees differ with changes in survey designs. Following is a brief summary of recent past and current methods used to calculate stocking and to estimate forest-type and stand-product (stand-size) classes.

Current fixed-radius tree tally—Currently, stand-product and forest-type classifications are based on a computation of stocking from tallied trees by forest condition. Observations recorded include a seedling (<1.0-inch d.b.h.) count, a tally of all-live trees 1.0 to 4.9 inches d.b.h. on a 6.8-foot radius microplot, and a tally of all-live trees ≥5.0 inches d.b.h. for each 24-foot radius plot.

Previous variable and fixed-radius tree tally—FIA surveys conducted from the 1970s to the mid-1990s based forest-type and stand-product (stand-size) classifications on a computation of stocking for tallied trees from a maximum of 10 sample points per forest land location. Trees 1.0 to 4.9 inches d.b.h. were tallied on a 6.8-foot radius microplot. Trees ≥5.0 inches d.b.h. were selected with a 37.5-BAF prism sample. Seedlings (<1.0-inch d.b.h.) were tallied only if no larger trees were present.

Forest type—Forest type is based upon and named for the tree species that forms the plurality of live-tree stocking if at least 10 percent is stocked with live trees.

Hardwoods and softwoods are first aggregated to determine the predominant group, and forest type is selected from the predominant group. Eastern softwood groups have ≥50-percent softwood stocking and contain the named species that constitute a plurality of the stocking; the oak-pine group and hardwood groups have <50-percent softwood stocking. The nonstocked group includes stands <10-percent stocked with live trees.

The current fixed-radius inventory design identifies a forest type for each forest condition. Under the previous variable-radius sample design, forest type was assigned to the entire plot.

Stand-product (size) class—Stand-product class is a computed classification of forest land based on the diameter class distribution of live trees in the stand. The current fixed-radius inventory design assigns a stand-product class for each forested condition. The previous variable-radius sample design assigned a single stand-product class for the entire plot.

Estimating volume—Currently, FIA computes tree volume using a simple linear regression model (D^2H) that predicts gross cubic-foot volume inside bark from a 1-foot stump to a 4-inch upper diameter outside bark for each sample tree based on d.b.h. (D) and total height (H). Separate equation coefficients for southern tree species or species groupings, developed from standing and felled-tree volume studies conducted across several Southern States, are used. Volume in forks or limbs outside of the main bole is excluded.

FIA derives net cubic-foot volume by subtracting a field crew estimate of rotten or missing wood for each sample tree. Volume of the saw-log portion (expressed in International ¼-inch board feet and in cubic feet) of sample trees is computed using board foot/cubic foot ratio equations.

Previous inventory methods used to estimate tree volumes differed from those described above. FIA derived tree volume from several measurements on each tree tallied on forested sample plots. These measurements included d.b.h., bark thickness, total height, bole length, log length, and (depending upon the State being inventoried) up to four upper-stem diameters that defined pole top, pole mid, saw top, and saw mid.

Gross tree volumes (cubic- and board-foot values) were determined by applying the formula for a conic frustum to sections of the bole. The volumes of the sections were then added together to produce a total stem volume.

Obtaining net cubic-foot volume involved subtracting a field crew estimate of rotten or missing wood for each sample tree. Merchantable volume was calculated from measurements of the bole from a 1-foot stump to an upper-stem stopping point determined by merchantability standards. The upper-stem diameter at this point could be as low as 4 inches, but often was larger depending upon the perceived condition and product merchantability of the upper tree bole.

Because of these differences in volume computation and merchantability standards, previously reported volumes are not directly comparable to those reported in the current inventory. Previous tree volumes were recomputed using current equations for comparison. On average, the recomputed values were higher than the original volumes for both softwood and hardwood species. The revisions are greater for hardwood species than softwoods and greater for large diameter trees.

Estimating growth, removals, and mortality—One of the primary reasons for conducting forest inventories is to determine how much wood volume currently resides in southern forest stands, and to identify how and why it is changing. Estimates of growth, removals, and mortality provide some of the information needed to understand changes in volume.

Volume change components are derived from data collected during the remeasurement of sample plots established in the previous inventory. For previous inventories (plot design based on a cluster of 10 prism points established at intervals of 66 feet), trees ≥5.0 inches d.b.h. at each prism point were selected with a 37.5-BAF prism. Trees <5.0 inches d.b.h. but ≥1.0-inch d.b.h. were tallied on three or more circular fixed plots, each of which was centered at one of the prism points. The center of prism point one and the center of subplot one in the new plot design are the same point.

Although the current and earlier plot designs may be judged statistically valid, the naturally occurring noise in the data hinders confident and rigorous trend assessments over time. When a design changes or plots are not remeasured, the true impact of such a change on trend analysis is unknown.

Growth estimation—Depending upon the State being inventoried, growth components were previously estimated using a Beers and Miller (1964) approach, or Beers and Miller as modified by Van Deusen and others (1986).

The two procedures differ in whether "ongrowth" trees on the prism plots are part of the growth components, and in how trees per acre are calculated. Both methods are known to be unbiased, but the inclusion of "ongrowth" trees can affect how growth is distributed among product classes that are defined in terms of tree size.

For the current inventories, the Beers and Miller method is used to estimate growth for all Southern States.